WOMEN CENTRE STAGE

HOW TO NOT SINK
Georgia Christou

WILDERNESS
April De Angelis

THE NIGHTCLUB
Chloe Todd Fordham

FUCKING FEMINISTS
Rose Lewenstein

TITUBA
Winsome Pinnock

THE ROAD TO HUNTSVILLE
Stephanie Ridings

WHITE LEAD
Jessica Siân

WHAT IS THE CUSTOM OF YOUR GRIEF?
Timberlake Wertenbaker

WOMEN CENTRE STAGE

Eight Short Plays by and About Women

www.nickhernbooks.co.uk   www.sphinxtheatre.co.uk

A Nick Hern Book

Women Centre Stage: Eight Short Plays By and About Women first published in Great Britain in 2018 as a paperback original by Nick Hern Books Limited, The Glasshouse, 49a Goldhawk Road, London W12 8QP, in association with Sphinx Theatre

Cover image: Camilla Harding, photographed by Deniz Guzel

Designed and typeset by Nick Hern Books, London
Printed in the UK by Mimeo Ltd, Huntingdon, Cambridgeshire PE29 6XX

A CIP catalogue record for this book is available from the British Library

ISBN 978 1 84842 769 3

Contents

Introduction	vii
Biographies	xii
Original Production Details	xvi
How to Not Sink by Georgia Christou	1
Wilderness by April De Angelis	17
The Nightclub by Chloe Todd Fordham	31
Fucking Feminists by Rose Lewenstein	43
Tituba by Winsome Pinnock	57
The Road to Huntsville by Stephanie Ridings	73
White Lead by Jessica Siân	105
What is the Custom of Your Grief? by Timberlake Wertenbaker	121

For My Comrades-in-Arms
Dame Rosemary Squire DBE and Jules Wright

And for Louisa, Tiffany, Helen, Ros,
Isabel, Lisa, Ben and Joanna.

Introduction

Sue Parrish

> 'Women can't be artists, women are mothers'
> *Sian Ede, Arts Council officer, 1991*

The eight plays in this volume first saw the light of day in the Women Centre Stage Festival. They were chosen to show the range, depth and richness of the work that can be created in a celebration of women artists. The Women Centre Stage Festival is an exciting cultural project designed to address and combat women's exclusion from UK theatre. Sphinx Theatre, founded as the Women's Theatre Group in 1973 and renamed in 1990, has been in the vanguard of advocating and inspiring women in the arts through productions, conferences and research for four decades. As a kind of feminist-theatre think tank, we initiated the breakthrough Glass Ceiling conferences in the 1990s at the National Theatre, and more recently from 2009, four Vamps, Vixens and Feminists conferences; while landmark productions include Pam Gems' *The Snow Palace* and April De Angelis' modern classic, *Playhouse Creatures*.

The conferences were a forum for gathering a UK-wide network and forming a sense of solidarity among women in the arts who are often isolated. Leading women artists, academics and journalists shared their professional experiences with packed audiences. For ten years running we hired the NT's Cottesloe Theatre for the day for the Glass Ceilings, and in 2009, thanks to the good offices of the Literary Manager Sebastian Born, we took over the Olivier Theatre for Vamps, Vixens and Feminists, a sign of dawning consciousness. Many women recount moments of inspiration from these talkshops, and the latest spin-off, Nottingham's The Party Somewhere Else, took its name from a passing reference of mine to the feeling of exclusion women feel.

However, by 2012 I was haunted by a feeling of extreme
Groundhog Day, bearing in mind that I had been involved in
campaigning for equality for women in the theatre for over
thirty-five years without feeling we'd made much progress. Yes,
there had been some improvement since then for women
directors and writers, but the figures for female actors remained
stubbornly at around 35%. The most recent figures show
women writers with work produced at 28%, directors at 36%,
and actors at 39%, but nowhere approaching parity for the 51%
of the population who are the only majority with the status of a
minority. The data shows that out of one hundred and sixty-
eight Artistic Directors of Arts Council England's National
Portfolio clients, only thirty-three are women, and they control
only 13% of the total ACE theatre budget. Women Centre Stage
was created to address this exclusion, at a time when the
murmuring for quotas is ever louder.

Sphinx Theatre has always had a feminist vision committed to
changing the cultural landscape. We were convinced that if
women artists were given space and support they could develop
and expand the range of representation of women onstage
beyond the endemic cultural stereotypes of wife, mother,
mistress, daughter, sister or girlfriend to the male protagonist.
We were confident that women could write 'state of the nation'
plays, away from the domestic arena. We were fired by the
passion and the quality of artists we met through our
discussions. Finally, in 2014, after several rejections, the Arts
Council made an award for the project.

Women Centre Stage, Heroines, began with an invitation from
the NT in 2014 to occupy the Temporary Theatre Space (aka the
National Theatre Shed) on the South Bank for a weekend in
2015. We had to move fast to get the funding and the
programme in place. This offer kickstarted five months of
writers' workshops, submissions, regional collaborations, panel
discussions and an initial hothouse meeting which brought
together women and men across the arts and education. We
developed a writers' programme of 'prompts and provocations';
examining classic texts alongside contemporary responses; and
salon discussions exploring the creation of female characters

who have agency, autonomy within the story, authority as protagonists, and authenticity as complex characters. The Sphinx Test (a tool we developed inspired by the film industry's Bechdel Test) and an alternative way of thinking about a female protagonist, took shape alongside – it is reproduced on the inside cover of this book. The festival exceeded all our objectives, and delivered the essential elements of any work of art: surprise and enlightenment!

The Temporary Theatre space was a provisional, rough and neutral space admirably suited to the festival spirit. The event was a euphoric success which brought a new and enthusiastic demographic into the NT for a range of pieces; including for Kali Theatre's searing dissection of oppression in *Twelve Women*; Hot Tubs and Trampolines' heart-stopping examination of grief in *Mind The Gap*; Lucinka Eisler's mesmerising presentation of old age in *A Life in 22 Minutes*; the shocking exposé of the power of social media, *Boys Will Be Boys* from Charlotte Josephine; and the chilling verbatim play *Islands* by Emma Jowett, documenting violent stalking. Bolton Octagon brought two elegant and elegiac pieces from Timberlake Wertenbaker: *What is the Custom of Your Grief?* and *Memory of Gold*. There were wonderful comedic pieces including *Prepper* by Caroline Moran, brilliantly performed by Abi Tedder; and Karen Featherstone's school-gate farce, *The Real PTA*. Three of the most stunning minutes were created by Camilla Harding, in her *Guy is a Guy*, inhabiting a Stepford Wife dancing to Doris Day, and morphing into a slobby young man before our eyes. To crown the day there were five twenty-four-hour plays, brilliantly diverse, from Roy Williams, April De Angelis, Barney Norris, Rachel De-Lahay and Rona Munro (who emailed her script from 30,000 feet en route across the Atlantic). But who could forget Tricia Kelly as Barney's unctuous C of E Bishop?

With a day's preparation, the NT crew worked miracles to enhance with sound and lighting twenty-four plays, created by seventy-one actors, twenty-four directors and twenty-six writers. It was an exhilarating experimental festival, bringing together experienced playwrights and new writers who were graduating from workshops, pub stages and studio theatres; creating dynamic plays with women as the focus; enticing 1,000 people through the doors; and turning the world upside down!

The second Women Centre Stage Festival, Powerplay, was held in November 2016, at the warm invitation of Edward Hall, Artistic Director of Hampstead Theatre. This offered the challenge and opportunity of a sophisticated main stage, a studio and a rehearsal space, facilitating an expanded festival with a range of performances, and with enhanced funding. We were concerned that the presentations should be as finished as possible in this super-modern theatre. Several pieces from the NT were further developed, and have since gone on to tour and be performed at other events. Again we were delighted to bring leading writers and directors together with emerging talents, through our writers' group, and the twenty-four-hour plays. We were able to offer extended rehearsal for two major new pieces – *Wilderness* by April De Angelis, and *Tituba* by Winsome Pinnock – and development time for Camilla Harding's *Guy is a Guy*, which became *Man Up*; and a second performance for plays premiered at the Bush Theatre, Theatre503 and Birmingham Rep. Joining the Hiccup Project on the main stage, a new collaboration with Graeae's women writers yielded a stunning *What I Was Told I Could Be & What I've Become*, which was a new departure for them; and Tanika Gupta's *A Perfect Match* came from Stratford East. The twenty-four-hour plays, triggered as in 2015 by newspaper headlines, produced star performances from Beatie Edney, Stella Gonet, Maggie Steed and Ann Mitchell for, respectively, Rebecca Lenkiewicz, Vinay Patel, Charlene James and Howard Brenton. With packed audiences across the three auditoria, Hampstead was buzzing! The collective anticipation of new stories, characters and experiences was palpable all day, and crowned by Dame Janet Suzman and Kathryn Pogson's performances of the comic and earthy *Wilderness* earning a standing ovation; and the electric performance by Cecilia Noble of *Tituba*. One hundred and thirty-two artists took part: over seven hours of performances there were twenty-five plays, four workshops and a panel discussion.

Both of these Women Centre Stage Festivals fizzed with creativity, providing opportunities for showcasing and networking among artists and programmers, and showing that there is a wealth of talent ready to rise to the challenge of making brilliant theatre for main stages. They were designed to work as immersive events, so the impact was cumulative.

There are upwards of seventy young women's theatre groups subsisting on crumbs from the funding table. There needs to be a redistribution of opportunity and funding to bring leading women writers and directors, and emerging talents to our main stages. This anthology is one more attempt to rectify the gender balance. I hope you will enjoy these plays as much as we did at their creation.

London
May 2018

Sue Parrish is the Artistic Director of Sphinx Theatre.

Biographies

GEORGIA CHRISTOU

Georgia Christou took part in Young Writers' Programmes at the Royal Court Theatre and the Lyric Hammersmith. Her debut play *Yous Two* was shortlisted for the Verity Bargate Award and was produced at Hampstead Theatre Downstairs in 2018. Other theatre includes: *How To Spot An Alien* (Paines Plough/Theatre Clwyd) and *Rocket Girl* (Royal Central School of Speech and Drama/Minack Theatre). She has also written short plays for DryWrite, Bush and Sphinx Theatre. TV includes: *Through the Gates* (Channel Four/Blacklight TV). She has original ideas for television in development with HillBilly films and Various Artists Ltd.

APRIL DE ANGELIS

April De Angelis is an acclaimed writer whose extensive theatre work includes *My Brilliant Friend*, a two-part dramatisation of Elena Ferrante's epic family saga (Rose Theatre Kingston); *After Electra* (Theatre Royal Plymouth and Tricycle Theatre 2015); *Rune* (New Vic Theatre Stoke 2015); *Gastronauts* (Royal Court Upstairs, 2013); *Jumpy* (Royal Court 2011and Duke of York's Theatre 2012, Melbourne and Sydney 2015); an adaptation of *Wuthering Heights* (Birmingham Rep, 2008); *A Laughing Matter* (Out of Joint at National Theatre, 2001); *A Warwickshire Testimony* (RSC, 1999); *The Positive Hour* (Out of Joint at Hampstead Theatre, 1997); *Playhouse Creatures* (Old Vic Theatre, 1993; revived at Chichester Festival Theatre in 2013); and *The Life and Times of Fanny Hill* (The Old Fire Station Oxford, 1991; revived at the Bristol Old Vic, 2015). Her new adaptation of *Frankenstein* opened at the Royal Exchange Theatre, Manchester in Spring 2018. Current work includes commissions for the Royal & Derngate Northampton and BBC Radio 4.

CHLOE TODD FORDHAM

Chloe Todd Fordham is an award-winning playwright from London. Her play *Sound of Silence* won a Bruntwood Prize Judges Award in 2015. Her play *The Next Generation* was shortlisted for the 2017 Writers in Theatre Award, run by Out of Joint. Her first play *Land's End* was developed while studying at Goldsmiths University and through the the Arcola's inaugural PlayWROUGHT festival, and was later shortlisted for Theatre503's Playwriting Award in 2014. Short plays include: *The Nightclub* (originally commissioned by MamaQuilla as part of Acts of Defiance at Theatre503, later developed for Sphinx's Women Centre Stage Festival at Hampstead Theatre), *Play 9* (for PLAY Theatre Company, Vault Festival), *Chicken and Chips*, part of EleXion (Theatre503). Chloe is a graduate of the 503Five, Theatre503's writer residency scheme and has attended the Kenyon College Playwrights Conference in Ohio (supported by Bruntwood and the Royal Exchange). She has an MA in Writing for Performance from Goldsmiths University. Chloe currently also works as the Literary Manager at Graeae Theatre Company.

ROSE LEWENSTEIN

Rose Lewenstein's plays include: *Darknet* (Southwark Playhouse); *Psychoslut* (Women@RADA); *Now This Is Not The End* (Arcola); *Game of Life* (The Yard); *Only Human* (Theatre503) and *Ain't No Law Against Fish 'n' Chips* (Royal Court Young Writers Festival). She is currently under commission to the Royal Court and is developing original TV dramas with Kudos, Hillbilly, SunnyMarch and BlackLight/Channel 4.

WINSOME PINNOCK

Winsome Pinnock is a playwright and academic who was born in London to parents who were both migrants from Jamaica. Her theatre credits include: *The Principles of Cartography* (Bush Theatre); *Tituba* (Hampstead Theatre); *Cleaning Up*, *Taken* (Clean Break at Ovalhouse Theatre); *IDP, One Under, Water* (Tricycle Theatre); *The Stowaway* (Plymouth Theatre);

Beg Borrow or Steal (Kuumba Community Arts Centre); *Mules, Water, A Hero's Welcome, A Rock in Water* (Royal Court); *Can you Keep a Secret?* (NT Connections); *Leave Taking* (Liverpool Playhouse Theatre; revived at Bush Theatre in 2018); *The Wind of Change* (Half Moon Theatre); *Picture Palace* (Women's Theatre Group). Radio plays include: *Clean Trade* (Radio 4); *Lazarus* (BBC Radio 3); *Her Father's Daughter* (BBC Radio 4); *Let Them Call it Jazz* (adapted from Jean Rhys' short story, BBC Radio 4); *Indiana* (adapted from novel by George Sand); *The Dinner Party* (BBC Radio 4); *Something Borrowed* (BBC Radio 4) and *Water* (BBC Radio 4). She co-wrote the screenplay *Bitter Harvest*. Awards include: the George Devine Award, Pearson Plays on Stage Scheme Best Play of the Year Award, Unity Trust Theatre Award. She was also runner-up for the Susan Smith Blackburn Prize. She was Senior Visiting Fellow at Cambridge University and Writer in Residence at Holloway Prison, Clean Break Theatre Company, Royal Court Theatre, Kuumba Arts Community Centre, Tricycle Theatre, and the National Theatre Studio. She is currently Associate Professor at Kingston University.

STEPHANIE RIDINGS

Stephanie Ridings is a writer and performer based in the West Midlands. *The Road to Huntsville* received a Bitesize commission in 2015; after opening at the Edinburgh Fringe 2016 and winning an Arts Voice award, the work toured throughout 2017. Her recent and most notable work has been *Dylan's Parents* for Live Lunch at the Royal Court. and *Unknown Male*, Birmingham REP, which was the winner of the Peter Brook/Mark Marvin award. Her first major script, *Me, Mum & Dusty Springfield*, enjoyed a sell-out Edinburgh Festival and went on to be supported by The Lowry (Salford) and tour nationally. She has been Artist in Residence at Contact Theatre (Manchester) and has been commissioned to write for a range of companies including Women and Theatre, Birmingham REP's Learning and Participation, Corby Young Actors at the Core at Corby and a radio play for Cotesbach Trust, Leicestershire.

JESSICA SIÂN
Jessica Siân is an actor and playwright, her debut play *Klippies* was nominated for an OFFIE for Most Promising New Playwright. She was commissioned by Southwark Playhouse to adapt *Kiki's Delivery Service*, which was remounted in summer 2017 after a sell-out Christmas run. She is a Royal Court Young Writers alumnus and her work has been supported by the National Theatre Studio and the Almeida. She has been commissioned by Southwark Playhouse, the Bush Theatre and Sphinx Theatre for their Hampstead Theatre Take Over.

TIMBERLAKE WERTENBAKER
Timberlake Wertenbaker grew up in the Basque country and lives in London. She is one of the UK's leading playwrights and her work is performed worldwide. She is the recipient of numerous awards including an Olivier Award and the New York Drama Critics' Award for *Our Country's Good* and a Writers' Guild Award for *Three Birds Alighting On A Field*. *Jefferson's Garden* won the 2016 Writers' Guild Award for Best Play and opened in Washington in January 2018. Other plays include: *Winter Hill*, *My Father*, *Odysseus*, *Magna Carta Plays*, *We Sell Right*, *Walking The Tightrope*, *The Ant and the Cicada*, *The Love of the Nightingale*, *Our Ajax*, *The Line*, *Galileo's Daughter*, *Credible Witness*, *The Break of the Day*, *The Grace of Mary Traverse*, *Abel's Sister*, *Ash Girl* and *After Darwin*. Translations include: *Britannicus*, *Antigone*, *Elektra*, *Hecuba*, *Wild Orchids*, *Jenufa*, *The Thebans* and *Mephisto*. Timberlake is currently working on a new commission for the Royal Shakespeare Company.

The first seven plays in this anthology were first performed at Hampstead Theatre, London, on 20 November 2016, with the following casts and creative teams:

HOW TO NOT SINK by Georgia Christou

The cast was as follows:

JOJO	Kirsty Adams
KIM	Zara Plessard
JEAN	Miranda Bell

Director	Helen Barnett

Commissioned and produced by Sphinx Theatre.

WILDERNESS by April De Angelis

The cast was as follows:

WOMAN	Janet Suzman
DOCTOR	Kathryn Pogson

Director	Susannah Tresilian

Commissioned and produced by Sphinx Theatre.

THE NIGHTCLUB by Chloe Todd Fordham

The cast was as follows:

BETTY	Marlene Sidaway
AMINA	Nita Mistry
HELEN	Karlina Grace-Paseda

Director	Lisa Cagnacci

Commissioned and produced by Theatre503 and Mama Quilla Productions.

FUCKING FEMINISTS by Rose Lewenstein

The cast was as follows:
Ania Sowinski
Jody Jameson
Karlina Grace-Paseda
Anna Elijas

Director   Lisa Cagnacci

Commissioned and produced by Theatre503 and Mama Quilla Productions.

TITUBA by Winsome Pinnock

The cast was as follows:
Cecilia Noble

Director   Winsome Pinnock

Commissioned and produced by Sphinx Theatre. The research and development of the piece was supported by a grant from the Peggy Ramsay Foundation. A shorter version of the show was first presented at the Women Centre Stage Festival in 2016, produced by Sue Parrish, with Cecilia Noble in the title role.

THE ROAD TO HUNTSVILLE by Stephanie Ridings

The cast was as follows:
Stephanie Ridings

Director   Jonathan V McGrath
Producer   Pippa Frith

Commissioned by China Plate, mac birmingham and Warwick Arts Centre. Supported by Arts Council England, Birmingham REP, The Sir Barry Jackson Trust and the Peggy Ramsay Foundation.

WHITE LEAD by Jessica Siân

The cast was as follows:
VENNI	Karen Bryson
DIDO	Jessica Sian
CAROL	Kirsty Bushell

Director   Chelsea Walker

Commissioned and produced by Sphinx Theatre.

WHAT IS THE CUSTOM OF YOUR GRIEF? by Timberlake Wertenbaker was first performed at the Octagon Theatre, Bolton, on 29th March 2015.

The cast was as follows:
EMILY	Anna Tierney
ZARGHONA	Nadia Clifford

Director   Elizabeth Newman

Commissioned and produced by the Octagon Theatre, Bolton, for the 2015 National Theatre Women Centre Stage.

Women Centre Stage supported by Arts Council England, Women's Playhouse Trust, The Unity Theatre Trust, Backstage Trust, David Teale Charitable Trust and Freemantle Media.

Special thanks to the National Theatre and Hampstead Theatre.

For Sphinx Theatre

Artistic Director   Sue Parrish
Associate Directors   Helen Barnett and Rosalind Philips

Women Centre Stage produced by Joanna Hedges
Production Manager   Heather Doole

Patrons   Beatrix Campbell OBE, Dame Janet Suzman DBE, Professor Janet Todd and Hélène Cixous

Board   Susan McGoun, Susannah Kraft-Levene, Ben Monks, Maggie Saxon, Jane Seymour

HOW TO NOT SINK

Georgia Christou

Characters

JOJO, *early twenties*
KIM, *early forties*
JEAN, *early sixties*

Scene One

Bedroom. JOJO *wears outdoor clothes. She is soaking wet.*

JOJO. Everyone goes for Chris at the start. Which I understand why, cos he's more stronger. But what people don't realise is that being strong doesn't actually mean you got a better chance of survival. Like in the first game, it's not even about being strong. It's about puzzles and keys and that, isn't it, I mean Chris don't even start with a gun. Mum. Did you hear that?

KIM *enters with a towel.*

KIM. Yep.

JOJO. He doesn't even start / with a gun.

KIM. With a gun, I know. What a dickhead.

JOJO. Would you go into Spencer Mansion without a gun?

KIM. Only if I was a dickhead.

JOJO. Exactly. That's why you're always best off playing as Jill –

KIM. JoJo.

JOJO. Cos she's not as strong –

KIM. Clothes.

JOJO. She's not as strong but she's well more clever.

KIM. Jo.

JOJO. What?

KIM. Come on.

JOJO. I am.

KIM. It's freezing.

JOJO. Alright stop going on.

KIM. Get your clothes off.

JOJO. Can I put Xbox on?

KIM. I'm not answering that.

JOJO. Mum!

KIM. –

JOJO. Can I? Can I or not?

KIM. –

JOJO. Can I though?

KIM. You're a grown-up, Jo.

JOJO. So can I?

KIM. Do what you want, just stop asking. And change your clothes.

    JOJO holds her arms out.

    Pause.

JOJO. Go on then.

    KIM *throws the towel at* JOJO*'s feet and exits.*

    JOJO *picks up the towel and rubs it over her head. She takes off her coat. Her clothes underneath are sodden too. She retrieves a plastic bag from the covers of her bed.*

    She looks at the door.

    Then hides the plastic bag again.

    KIM *enters.*

KIM. What you / doing?

JOJO. I didn't –

KIM. Get off the bloody bed.

JOJO. You're swearing at me.

KIM. You wanna sleep in wet sheets?

JOJO. Why you shouting?

KIM. You don't listen. How many times do I have to ask you to do the same thing over and over?

JOJO. You do it then.

KIM. I'm not undressing you. Just sheer laziness.

JOJO. You're meant to be looking after me.

KIM. Says who?

JOJO. Meant to take care of me.

KIM. Why am I?

JOJO. Cos.

KIM. Cos what?

JOJO. Cos, cos it's your job.

KIM. If it was my job I'd be paid, wouldn't I?

JOJO. Being horrible.

KIM. Holiday leave. Pension.

JOJO. Laughing at me.

KIM. Who's laughing?

JOJO. Everyone.

KIM. I'm not laughing.

JOJO. By the river.

KIM. Come here.

JOJO. They was laughing at me.

KIM. Don't get all –

JOJO. Taking the piss.

KIM. Try and forget it.

JOJO. They was though, Mum.

KIM *puts her hands together in front of her.*

I hate them.

JOJO *puts her hands together to meet* KIM*'s.*

KIM. I know.

They play slaps.

JOJO. Pigs.

KIM *goes for* JOJO. *Wins a point.*

KIM. Need to concentrate.

JOJO. I'll kill them –

KIM *goes for* JOJO, *wins another point.*

KIM. Come on.

JOJO *goes for* KIM, *misses.*

JOJO. You have to give me a chance.

KIM. No chances.

JOJO. You always give me a chance.

KIM. No more chances.

JOJO *goes for* KIM, *misses.*

Nearly.

JOJO *tries again, misses.*

I'm mullering you here.

JOJO *tries and misses.*

Tries and misses.

JOJO *hits* KIM *in the face.*

Pause.

JOJO. I want my inhaler.

Beat.

Mum.

Beat.

Want my inha–

KIM. Where'd you last have it?

JOJO. Dunno. You find it.

Beat.

You know Michaela's got a boyfriend? Did you know that, Mum? She met him down Waitrose. She's on the tills, he's on the trolleys. She's always showing off about him but I've seen him and he's nothing to write home about.

KIM *finds the inhaler in a bag.*

KIM. Listen to me. You have to keep this with you, okay? Yes, hello?

KIM *holds the inhaler to* JOJO*'s mouth.*

JOJO *goes to take a pump on it.*

KIM *pulls it away.*

Would you send Chris off on a campaign without any weapons?

She offers it again, pulls it away again.

Or without herbs? With an empty pack?

JOJO. I'm not insane.

KIM. Right. So you've got to make sure you've got your inventory on you, okay? Your pump.

JOJO. Mum!

KIM *holds the inhaler out of reach.*

KIM. Money –

JOJO. Give it –

KIM. Your mobile. All the stuff we've been talking about.

JOJO. Give it I said!

KIM. Survival pack.

JOJO. Don't be tight.

KIM. You need to learn your limits. Don't bite the hand that feeds you. You know what that means?

Beat.

It means don't hit me in the fucking face.

KIM *holds out the inhaler.* JOJO *takes a big pull on it.*

Kiss me.

They kiss on the lips.

Pause.

You smell like wet dog.

JOJO. 'Kay.

Pause.

KIM. You think Michaela could see if there's any jobs going down Waitrose?

JOJO. You wanna work there?

KIM. For you I mean.

JOJO. I don't think so.

KIM. Christmas job.

JOJO. Embarrassing.

KIM. Nothing embarrassing about having a bit of money in your pocket.

JOJO. You do it then.

KIM. Maybe I will.

JOJO. It's a piss-take.

KIM. It's John Lewis.

JOJO. I gotta stay focused anyway. Get training. So I can do army.

Beat.

KIM. We talked about army.

JOJO. I told you though. It ain't all about being strong. Is it? Is it, Mum?

KIM. Dunno.

JOJO. Are you actually getting a job though?

KIM. –

JOJO. You can't get a job, Mum.

KIM. Can do what I want.

JOJO. What am I gonna do then?

KIM. I don't know. That's your problem, isn't it.

Pause.

JOJO. Mum?

KIM. What snot shit in a pot.

JOJO. Bath.

KIM. Shit!

KIM *opens her eyes and jumps out of bed. Exits.*

JOJO *gets the bag out from the bed again. Inside is a game –* Resident Evil 7: Biohazard. *She sets up the Xbox.*

KIM *enters, watches* JOJO *for while.*

A zombie on the screen roars.

KIM *roars as well.*

JOJO. You made me –

KIM *roars again.*

Don't.

KIM *roars again.*

I don't like that.

KIM *roars again, closer this time.*

I'll shoot you.

JOJO *simulates shooting* KIM.

KIM *roars, closer.*

Stop it.

She changes her weapon, shoots again.

Stop it, Mum.

She changes her weapon, shoots again. KIM *is hit. She collapses, lifeless, on the floor.*

JOJO *edges closer. She bends close to* KIM.

KIM *suddenly wakes up, grabs* JOJO *by the arm.*

JOJO *screams.*

KIM. What did you forget?

JOJO. –

KIM. It's basics, Jo. When you make a kill what should you do?

JOJO. Burn the body.

KIM. Or what?

JOJO. You turn into a crimson head.

KIM. Why's the bath cold?

JOJO. What?

KIM. I need you to think about it.

JOJO. I'm trying.

KIM. Why's there no hot water? Are you going to answer me.

JOJO. You done the wrong tap.

KIM. No, no I didn't.

JOJO. I don't know I said.

KIM. The money I gave you yesterday, Jo, what was you supposed to use it for.

JOJO. Key.

KIM. See you do know. Told you to top up the meter, didn't I? And what did you spend it on? What did you buy instead?

JOJO. Game.

KIM. Yeah. Game.

KIM *lets go of* JOJO.

JOJO. Don't be annoyed, okay.

KIM. I'm trying –

JOJO. I'll get some / more money.

KIM. But it's like / the harder I –

JOJO. I'll get more.

KIM *(calm)*. From where though. Tell me? Because you don't have a job. And our money won't come in till Friday. So what are we gonna do between now and Friday?

JOJO. I'll get a scratchcard.

KIM. You're not listening again. I told you. I told you not to stand so close to the water. Are you gonna get undressed or not?

JOJO *puts her hands out to play slaps*.

KIM *puts her hands together*.

JOJO *tries for a point. Misses*.

JOJO *tries for a point. Misses*.

JOJO *tries for a point. Misses*.

  Go and get in.

JOJO. Get in where?

KIM. Go on.

JOJO. You gonna get my clothes off?

KIM. You have to learn.

JOJO. I don't want to.

KIM. You're gonna have to learn.

JOJO *exits.*

Scene Two

Middle of the night.

Dark apart from the light of a screen.

JOJO *still in her wet clothes, she holds the controller. The roar of zombies. She is shaking.*

JOJO (*shouts*). Mum.

She hits the keys.

Mum!

She hits the keys.

It's c–

She hits the keys.

I'm cold.

KIM *watches* JOJO.

Mum!

Blackout.

Scene Three

Hospital.

KIM *sits on a plastic chair.*

JEAN *wears pyjamas and a coat. She doesn't sit.*

KIM. We was up the top of the chalk pits, out the back of the old house. You don't...? You took me up there on my bike. Can only have been seven or eight. A birthday maybe, cos the bike was brand new. And I'd seen other kids around, being chased by a dad or whatever, holding on and falling down and trying again and I was ready for that and so when I started I thought you were there.

Felt like you was there.

It was only when I got down the bottom. I looked up and you was so high I couldn't even see your face properly. Was only then that I realised I'd been on my own.

Beat.

She's fine. Mild hypothermia. You look brown.

JEAN. Yes, alright.

KIM. I'm not being –

JEAN. I know what you're not being and you *are* being. So.

Beat.

KIM. How's Dean?

JEAN. I won't be made to feel guilty.

KIM. I wasn't –

JEAN. I had a nice time. Okay?

KIM. I'm glad.

JEAN. I enjoyed myself. You think I shouldn't?

KIM. I think life's too short.

JEAN. The weather was spectacular. I kicked back I really did. All-inclusive. Three different musicals. I laughed. I drank. *The Phantom of the Opera*, twice in ten days. It really was magnificent. Was all this for my benefit?

KIM. All this?

JEAN. A cry for attention, for help, whatever. My punishment, the first / holiday I've taken in –

KIM. Hypothermia, Mum.

JEAN. Quick, she's enjoying herself someone grab a hammer to nail her to the fucking cross.

KIM. Okay.

JEAN. Yes, okay.

Pause.

You know if it were my money it would be different. You know that, don't you?

KIM. I know.

JEAN. I'll ask him. If you want me to, if that's what it all boils down to, then I'll ask.

KIM. I don't want that.

JEAN. Well I've offered. Haven't I?

KIM. You've offered.

JEAN. So.

JEAN sits.

You look tired.

KIM. I'm not.

JEAN. You know I shook you when you was little.

KIM. Bloody hell, Mum.

JEAN. I did. Only once but even so. You never slept, nightmare, just screaming at me screaming and screaming. I wanted to smother your red little face sometimes.

KIM. Thanks.

JEAN. I'm just saying, it feels personal, doesn't it, when you're in it? Like you were doing it to spite me.

KIM. I was.

JEAN. Well yes I know that now.

Beat.

If someone had told me it was gonna go on forever. I only
did it once, but if someone had said...

KIM. Jo would sleep fifteen hours a day if I let her, the lazy sod.

JEAN. Well that's something at least.

KIM. It's not the same.

JEAN. I'm sure.

KIM. It's not, Mum.

JEAN. How long was she sitting in her clothes?

KIM. You can think what you want.

JEAN. How long, Kimberly?

KIM. I've spent twenty years and a fortune on dry snacks
keeping her alive.

JEAN. I don't mean –

KIM. You do. You do mean that so just say it.

Beat.

How she looked at me, Mum. I don't even know how long
she was in there, but I could see her eyes, she had her eyes
on me all the time. Like this shock and expectation and...
She was doing it, I'm sure she was, experiencing something.
Keeping her head up, that's why I didn't...

Beat.

And then I just suddenly couldn't see her. These kids yanked
her out. You'd think something would kick in wouldn't you.
Instinct. But it doesn't. It didn't.

JEAN. I'm not having a go –

KIM. That's what someone says just before they're about to
have a go.

JEAN *receives a text.*

JEAN. Dean. Should he park up?

KIM. What's he been doing till now?

JEAN. Driving round the block. Six pound an hour.

KIM. Call you when we're home.

JEAN. It's no bother.

KIM. Go on.

JEAN. You know she'll be alright without you, if it comes to that, which it won't but if it does. She can't let you know that's all.

KIM. What d'you mean?

JEAN. It's like that with your kids. They always wait till you're not looking.

Scene Four

JOJO *stands by a river. She wears a new coat. There is a bag next to her on the ground. The sound of the water rushing beneath her. The river gets louder. She removes her shoes. She takes an inhaler from her bag. She takes a step closer. She closes her eyes. The river gets louder still.*

Black.

End.

WILDERNESS

April De Angelis

Character

A
B

1.

A   Need a bucket. Gonna puke

B   You're somatising

A   In the bin then

B   Directing hostility through the body

A   On the carpet? Had a Pop Tart for breakfast. Apricot.

B   That's full of tartrazine – a behaviour modifier – let's communicate

A   It's my weekend I've been looking forward to. They tell me this morning – oh there's been a change of plan – your leave cancelled. Smile on her like she grassed up Anne Frank.

B   Something happened didn't it?

A   Flossie picking me up at ten in the hatchback going to Frinton to walk her dogs. A big grey churning sea. Afterwards we're having chips.

        Going to vom now. Choose where. You got approximately ten seconds

B   Tell me about the faeces

A   –

B   Left outside my office –

A   In a cup

B   A breach of acceptable behaviour

A   That was Wednesday. *Since then I've been exemplary.*

        I never smeared it on your door handle

B   Disturbing

A   I could do your job – just hand out pills

B   I'm sure you could – if you'd spent seven years
      qualifying and twenty-five in clinical practice.

A   Flossie needs me – her dog's got liver cancer.

B   I know you're a sensible person and you'll understand
      that I'm following a protocol – a set of rules – we can
      reschedule your weekend – providing there are no
      other incidents

A   Bailey could be dead by then. She's liquidising his dog
      food now.

B   Because we're here to look after you, keep you safe.

A   Flossie's made him a little cart.

      A *begins to heave.*

      B *gets the bin.*

      A *throws up.*

      Sorry.

      Pause.

B   That's all right. I'm sure you couldn't help it.

A   It's going to be hard to get the stink out. I never told
      anyone.

      Pause.

B   Your shit is a little message saying – I'm not ready to
      go – we have to listen – you're here because we
      believe you may be a danger to yourself or others. I'd
      be letting you down if I let you go

A   I hallucinated.

      Went on all night. Dreamt I was in another place. My
      tongue swelled up. You gave me something extra.

B   I prescribed you paracetamol

A   This whole place is shit

B   You're being aggressive

A   Like a prison

        There was a reason I shat in that cup and we can call it
        quits if you let me have my weekend

B   I can't do that – a process has been set in motion which
        I can't override.

A   You gave me something – when everyone was off with
        norovirus and we were stressing about British Home
        Stores closing down.

        – you're in breach of your Hippocratic

B   That's a paranoid assumption.

        A *picks up the bin*.

A   I'm gonna make you eat this.

        B *sounds an alarm*.

2.

A   You're back

B   Yes

A   How was your holiday?

B   It wasn't a holiday

A   You were away from this place

B   Three days. I was on a professional development
        course

A   In the countryside – nice

B   I don't know if Croyden qualifies as the countryside

A   Meet any new people?

B   There were some fresh colleagues.

A   I'd love to have colleagues. They don't spit at you.

B   Not on the whole.

A   Not like the maniacs in here.

B   So I hear it's been rather eventful this last few days.

A   We had to think of a subject in the news to discuss – It
        all kicked off about Boris

B   Really?

A   Yeah. He can lie like a mad bastard but he's not in
        here. We're in here doing all the work to make people
        like him appear sane.

B   It's just a pity it ended in a violent altercation.

A   Some women find him attactive apparently.

B   A chair was broken.

A   That's life though. That's how everything ends.
        Bloodshed.

B   Not everything.

        And so group gatherings have been put on hold. I was
        hoping to try a few things out.

A   That's what your course was for.

        I know. I can read upside down.

        She gestures to desk.

        Hearing the voices; is the future drug-free?

        It's not going to work is it?

B   There have been some incredible results in Northern
        Lapland

A   Does that place actually exist?

B   Yes

        And the techniques they use have been very successful

        Pause.

So I thought – instead of this tedious unpicking of a
silly argument – we could try something.

A   Do I get my weekend away if I do it?

B   It's not a bribe.

The voices you get in your head – that's what I want to
hear about. You tell me what they say and we'll engage
with them

A   I try not to listen to them

B   This is a different approach.

A   It'll be a disaster.

B   Voices are not a disease but a response to troubling life
experiences.

Pause.

A   That's why I try to switch off.

B   Let's imagine we're both you. You speak for the voices
and I'll imagine I'm you responding.

Pause.

A   This is awful. It's like a play.

Pause.

You must go unto the wilderness!

B   The wilderness?

A   You must leave this place and go unto the wilderness

B   I'd like to know a bit more about the wilderness? What
is it?

A   It's the wilderness.

B   Do you know where the wilderness is

A   Well it is not Croydon.

B   No. Of course. So I presume you want me to go
somewhere that has not been significantly modified by
human activity

A   Yeah. Go you there and seek me, for you are she.

B   I am she – who is that

A   Holy. Divine. She

B   A goddess?

A   The wilderness could be Frinton-on-Sea

B   Isn't it possible that this voice of yours is telling you
      that you have a side that needs to be honoured.

A   It's nuts though, isn't it?

B   Is it? We push it away, we talk about delusion – but
      perhaps there is something divine in us? Something
      that when it isn't drugged and subdued and locked
      away is actually worthy of being honoured.

A   I suppose it's like – when I was a kid and I did a
      drawing of a warthog and I showed it to my mum and
      she said what the fuck is that – what have you
      scribbled on the A–Z – that was like crushing my spirit.

B   Yes.

A   She hid all my pencils.

B   Yes. That is right. Yes. Yes.

3.

The wilderness.

A   I've just been bitten.

B   I think there are midges around his time of year.

A   Little bastards.

B   They're not biting you intentionally.

A   They're too little to kill. You wouldn't even get any
      satisfaction out of killing anything that small.

B   I don't think we kill things for satisfaction.

A   Why else would you kill? It is nice here though.
        Frinton woods. I can hear birds.

B   It's peaceful.

A   You like it out of the office. You've unwound.

B   Yes.

A   It's like we're equal beings now. Adam and Eve. In
        paradise.

B   (*Unwrapping sandwiches*.) Egg or smoked salmon?

A   Egg.

B   So we've made progress.

        A *eats*.

        Would you agree

        A *nods*.

A   I'd rather be here without you

B   I accept that

A   That's my voices talking not me

B   But we know that your voices are you

A   Not really because I'd never say that.

B   Crisps?

A   I might think it.

        This isn't wilderness

B   Comparatively.

A   There's a tampon over in that bush. You'd never find
        one of them in the wilderness.

        Look what you've started. Words pouring out of me
        that I don't like.

B   That's fine.

A   For you. It's unnerving. You always in control.

B   I feel that over the past few weeks we've grown to trust each other. We've made some discoveries. You're cutting down on the meds. It's progress.

I feel I can trust you to hear something.

You were right. I did medicate you without prescription. I was very stressed. That's not an excuse just an explanation. Everything felt like it was on the brink of flying apart. I had a terrible headache. I'd sprained my ankle chasing after a patient who was experiencing a psychotic episode. We were short staffed. The norovirus! When you presented with manic-depressive symptoms I did something unprofessional and unacceptable. I gave you a fairly strong sedative.

A   Nitrazepam.

B   Yes.

A   I know. I did some research. You bitch.

B   Your voice is entitled to express anger.

A   So what you're admitting is the shit in the cup was justified.

B   Yes.

A   Should have done it in a saucepan.

B   I wanted to acknowledge my mistake because it was coming between us in the work.

So know I've given you information which you could use against me if you like. Now we're equals.

A   You know I'm not going to tell on you.

B   I wasn't sure.

A   Because I like you. Because who else have I got?

B   Your friend Flossie.

A   She's pissed off with me because I let her down –
        didn't turn up for the weekend. Also as we discussed
        what kind of person extends their identity into a
        canine? A neanderthal.

B   Let's just enjoy the day.

A   (*Re: sandwich.*) Bit of shell.

        Pause.

        So what kind of things do you do in your free time?

B   Well I belong to a book group.

A   Oh.

B   It's actually fun. We drink wine. We chat. It's very
        sociable.

A   Can I join your book group?

B   Would you want to? I didn't think you read books.

A   I can drink wine though.

        Pause.

        But I'd say something.

B   It's a very liberal atmosphere.

A   Yeah

B   It is.

A   Bet they've all got a mortgage.

B   Probably.

A   Bourgeois cunts.

B   You're right they wouldn't like that. I think that myself
        sometimes – after a really tough shift

A   But you'd never say it

B   Not if I wanted to come back.

A   So you lie.

B   Not really. Don't be so binary. It's just not appropriate to always tell the truth

A   But that's what you're telling me to do

B   Don't join a book group is my advice.

A   Oh how sensitive.

B   I haven't repressed my angry voice – I've accommodated it. That's what you'll learn to do in time. Perhaps.

A   I don't want to do that

B   Fine

A   I don't want to be a hypocrite like you. I'd rather fuck Donald Trump

B   I know this outing has an informal spirit about it but let's not go over the top

A   I tell you what I think of you – you blame us.

B   I don't

A   – for all the shit we bring down on you – what a headache we are – if only we behaved ourselves if only we weren't such head-fucks you could drink your nice wine and chat your nice chat and live in your nice properties if only there weren't vermin like us

B   Vermin – that is your voice

A   No it's yours.

B   You're very angry – calm down

A   Come unto the wilderness.

B   Put down the cheese knife

A   Don't you know we're not allowed knives?

B   Please put it down.

A   The goddess says fuck off.

     She holds the knife to her own wrist.

She says say after me

What she says is true

B   What she says is true

A   You are like our voices.

B   You are like our voices

A   We don't want to hear you

B   We don't want to hear you.

A   We push you away

B   We push you away

A   We drug you

B   We drug you

A   Then take you into the forest littered with sanitary products

B   I'm not saying that

Digs knife in.

A   Because we are weak and selfish

B   Because we are weak and selfish

A   Thank you.

B   Thank you.

A   No you don't have to say that. That was me.

End.

THE NIGHTCLUB

Chloe Todd Fordham

For all the LGBT+ people around the world

Characters

BETTY, *eighty-five*
HELEN, *fifty-two*
AMINA, *twenty-one*

Note on casting: please cast inclusively. Actively consider actors who identify as D/deaf and/or disabled and consider actors regardless of race and class.

Orlando, Florida.

June 12, 2016.

AMINA. Things you need to know about me. My name's
Amina. I'm twenty-one years old. I have a brother called
Gabeen. I'm majoring in Politics so I can be the first female
American-Pakistani President of the United States. My
favourite Hershey's is Cookies and Cream Kisses, Bean
prefers Reese's Peanut Butter Cups. (*Slight pause.*) Bean.
That's what I call my brother. What I've always called my
brother since, like, when we were in the womb. I'm a
Muslim. Kind of. Bean's more into it than I am but –

HELEN. My name's Helen Taylor. I live on Avalon Boulevard
with my husband, Carlton. He's a real-estate investment
property manager. We have two dogs. Bush and Clinton.
Bush has a urinary tract infection. The vet thinks we might
have to put him down, which is just tragic. We have one
daughter. Jessica. She's twenty-five. She doesn't live with us
any more. (*Slight pause.*) I want to tell you it was different
but it was pretty much identical to the movies. 'Mom, Dad...
sit down. There's something I need to tell you.' And then no
one sits down, because – well, you know how there's some
news that's better received on your feet so you can sit down,
and some news that's better received sitting down so you can
jump up? Her exact words were: 'I hate you. I don't want
anything to do with you ever again. Don't try to find me.'
There was more, but those are the lines that... stick.

BETTY. Betty Lorraine Sanderson. Married for sixty years to
Harold Sanderson, a trucker from Pennsylvania. We met in
1949 in a gas station in Jacksonville. He was taking
Westinghouse dishwashers to Miami from Detroit and I was
serving cheese grills in the diner. He told me he'd travelled
the length and breadth of the United States but he'd never
been made a cheese grill so good, and was I free next Friday
when he'd be taking Hoovers from Dallas to Orlando? I said

yes, made him another cheese grill and we were hitched within the year. (*Slight pause.*) It's hard to know… when you've only 'done it' with the one person… if it's them or if it's you. But I guess I knew deep down. Deep down, I've always known.

***

BETTY. / June 12 2016

AMINA. / June 12 2016

HELEN. June 12 2016

BETTY. It's coming up to 10 p.m.

AMINA. Weird I know but I have it in my head that if I don't tell him before 10 p.m. then I'll never tell him. My brother. Gabeen.

HELEN. It's always worse late at night

AMINA. And I'm watching the clock… 9.57… 9.58… 9.59…

BETTY. And I'm thinking to myself, when the big hand gets to the twelve that's going to be exactly seventy-two hours since my husband died.

AMINA. 'Hey Bean…?' 'Yeah' he goes.

HELEN. Except tonight it's worse than worse because it's three years, to the day, since the last time I saw her

AMINA. 'There's something I got to tell you.'

BETTY. Sixty years together and seventy-two hours apart… that's –

AMINA. 'I think I might be…' No going back now…

HELEN. Jessica

AMINA. 'I think I might be…'

HELEN. My daughter.

AMINA. 'Gay. I think I might be gay.'

***

AMINA. I slam the front door

HELEN. I start up my laptop

BETTY. I go to the garage. It smells of gasoline and damp and cigarettes and summer snapdragons

HELEN. And I wish I had given my daughter a more original name like Trig or Track or Kestral! Because there are fifteen thousand six hundred and seventy-eight other Jessica Taylors on Facebook… That's half the population of Pine Hills!

BETTY. Hose… sprinkler… plant pots… light bulbs… our old mattress… a heap of unpaid bills… old cigarette packets…

AMINA. My mom's Toyota Yaris is in the drive.

HELEN. I'm never going to find her.

BETTY. Paint! / Bingo!

AMINA. Bingo. I turn the key in the ignition. Gabeen thinks I should be – ? Handbrake up then down. Gabeen thinks I should be – ? Check rear-view mirror. Check wing mirrors. He thinks his sister should be – ?

BETTY. I take the paint cans one by up to my bedroom. Not easy at eighty-five! (*Laughs.*)

AMINA. He thinks his *twin* sister should be…?!

BETTY. I go to my wardrobe, I take out my wedding dress, I unzip it from its dust cover.

AMINA. I reverse out of the drive and into the night

BETTY. And onto my wedding dress… I paint the colours of the rainbow. Big rainbow stripes all the way down the front and back. Red and yellow and pink and green… (*Laughs.*)

AMINA. Left down Delaney Avenue… Right down Michigan Street… Left down Center Avenue, right down Jersey Street… and I wonder how far I'd get… turning right and left like this… until the anger goes away. Georgia? Montana? Alaska?

HELEN. One thousand, five hundred and eighty-nine Jessica Taylors down and bingo! There she is! She's cut her hair.

And she's… is that a nose piercing?! I scroll through her pictures and then her wall.

BETTY. When the paint dries, I get naked.

HELEN. She's attending an event tonight…

BETTY. I glimpse myself in the mirror. My body is smaller and saggier than I remember, but it's still me.

HELEN. An event… near me?

BETTY. A new me.

AMINA. Alaska.

BETTY. I step into my rainbow wedding dress.

***

BETTY. I don't know if it's my eyes or my legs but every man and woman on Orange Avenue is looking at me. (*Smiles*.)

AMINA. I'm on the corner of Orange Avenue and Esther Street and nothing is moving.

HELEN. I must have been walking for over an hour now. Where *is* this place?

BETTY. Every man… and *woman*.

AMINA. I press the horn. I shout at the traffic. I type Alaska into the GPS. 'You are four thousand, seven hundred and five miles from your destination.' FUCK!

BETTY. A young man in a Bernie Sanders baseball cap stands up through his sun roof and gives me a 'High-five, lady! Looking good!' He's right. I am looking good. For an eighty-five-year-old woman, dressed in a rainbow wedding dress, on her way to a gay disco. (*Smiles*.) If Harold could see me now…!

HELEN. Bush 'makes friends' with a lamp post and Clinton… he's giving me this look… like… 'give up' he's saying… 'give up, you homophobe'.

AMINA. Bean buried me once in West Palm Beach. We must have been five. The cold wet of the sand… the weight of the sand on my chest. Don't cry. Whatever you do, don't…

HELEN. One more block to go.

AMINA. I cry. Big fat belly sobs.

HELEN. What if she's not there? What if I don't recognise her? What if she's... *with* someone? What if she says it all again?

AMINA. When I dry my eyes... there's this old madwoman crossing in front of me. Wait, is that... paint? This dude in a Bernie Sanders baseball cap puts his head through the sun roof and whoops at her. She whoops him back. The courage... to have the courage... to just – !

***

AMINA. Before I know it, I'm parked up on Orange Avenue

HELEN. I tie my sanctimonious Shih Tzus to a bench. CLINTON! HEEL, BOY!

AMINA. And I'm heading for the nightclub

HELEN. And I head for the nightclub

BETTY. I make some wonderful new friends in the queue. There's Jerry, he's come as a German porn star. Joey, he's come as a Mexican. And Patricia... she's come as a man called Barry, dressed as a woman. 'Hey Betty... I hope you've brought your ID' she says (*Laughs. Pause.*) God rest her soul.

HELEN. I scan the queue for my daughter.

AMINA. How long's the wait? I ask the bouncer. She's got this tattoo on her face of a lizard eating a cockroach eating a dead mouse. 'You got ID?'

HELEN. 'Looking for someone?' this man in a sombrero asks.

AMINA. I get out my driver's licence. 'You sure you're in the right place?'

HELEN. I nod.

AMINA. I nod.

HELEN. 'They cis male, trans male, cis female, trans female?' Sombrero asks

AMINA. She eyeballs me. I smile.

HELEN. I smile. 'Sorry, I... I don't speak Spanish.' Sombrero takes my hand. His hands are soft and his pupils are – Is he... is he flirting with me?! 'Come inside' he says.

AMINA. 'Cloakroom to the left' she says. I'm in!

***

Music.

HELEN. It's huge.

AMINA. The place is massive.

HELEN. And it smells of... it smells of... (*Whispering.*) semen

BETTY. 'How does it feel to be the youngest person in the room?' Patricia asks me.

HELEN. I try to think of the last time I smelled semen.

AMINA. I'm the youngest person in here by about a decade

HELEN. West Palms, summer 2010?

AMINA. I'm going to need a drink.

HELEN. Jacksonville, fall 2007?

BETTY. I'm going to need a drink.

HELEN. I'm going to need a drink.

***

HELEN. I start with the dance floor

BETTY. Patricia asks me if I'd like to dance. I love a good dance.

HELEN. She always loved dancing as a kid

AMINA. I need to – get it out my system... the anger, the weight of the sand on my chest... I need... I need to move, dance

HELEN. I weave my way through the crowds.

BETTY. I'm parting the crowds like Moses parted the Red Sea!

HELEN. The floor is sticky with... surely not... !? (*Gasps*.) A soft hand touches my behind... sombrero

BETTY. I feel... magnificent.

HELEN. A man in leather grinds up against my leg

BETTY. I feel fabulous.

HELEN. A woman in a dog collar shows me her tongue.

BETTY. I feel alive.

HELEN. Where *is* she?

AMINA. There are these two girls on the dance floor... making out and... yeah it's... it's – I've never actually seen two women kiss before so... it looks... nice.

BETTY. There are these two women on the dance floor with their tongues down each other's throats. And it occurs to me. I'm eighty-five years old and I've only ever kissed one person. A man! I think to myself... that is the funniest thing I have ever heard. (*Laughs*.) My life is the funniest thing I have ever heard in all my life!

HELEN. There are these two 'cis' women on the dance floor... and they're... well it's... enthusiastic... and I'm trying not to look... no! not because I'm a – I'm not a – ! I'm trying to give them their privacy. Out of respect. One of them has short hair – Jessie? Is that you? I linger... wait for them to... come up for air... so I can get a look... 'Jessie?'

AMINA. A girl with a mohawk taps me on the shoulder. 'Hi' she shouts.

HELEN. Sorry, I didn't mean to... interrupt.

AMINA. 'Hi' I shout back. 'Nice lips.' 'Thanks.' (*Smiles*.) 'I'll show you mine' she says... pointing to her crotch. This is a mistake. / This whole thing is a – .

HELEN. This is a mistake. This whole thing is a –

AMINA. I should go... / I should just... go... home

HELEN. I should just... go... home

AMINA. to Gabeen and – .

HELEN. But before I know it I'm shouting. JESSICA?
JESSIE?

BETTY. There's this woman next to me shouting… she's high
as a kite!

HELEN. JESSIE BABY, IT'S MOM! I'M HERE. I'VE COME
TO FIND YOU. I'M SORRY BABY. I'M SORRY!

BETTY. I start to laugh. I laugh at my life until I cry, and then I
cry until I laugh and when I can't laugh any more… when I
can't laugh any more…

The music gets louder.

(*Smiling.*) I dance.

BETTY *starts to dance*.

AMINA. I push past the people on the dancefloor. Past the girl
with the mohawk and the man in the sombrero and the
kissing girls and the cold wet of the sand… the weight of the
sand on my chest on my neck in my mouth, I can't breathe! I
can't – ! I stop. (*Pause.*) There she is! The old madwoman in
the wedding dress. Her arms raised above her head, her hips
swinging, her smile as wide as Alaska. I watch her. She has
this thing… I want it more than anything else in the world…
more than a Hershey's Cookies and Cream Kiss… more than
to major in Politics, more than Gabeen. And this thing she
has… is freedom.

AMINA *starts to dance*.

HELEN. I'm about to give up when I see the weirdest thing. A
girl, about Jessie's age… and this woman… about my
mother's age… in a… is that a – ? I watch them. I'm
transfixed. It's something about the way they're moving.
Clumsy – like they're discovering dancing for the first time
but also – committed – like if they stop dancing a hurricane
will rip right through the nightclub and wipe us all out. It's
not just dancing… it's more than dancing… they're dancing
for something. I watch them some more. And as the music
gets more passionate, so does their dancing… and as their

dancing gets more passionate, the more I feel the urge to –
not to stop them – but to – the urge rising in me to… to…

HELEN *starts to dance.*

The music gets louder.

The three women dance… and dance… and dance.

Gunshots.

White noise.

Silence.

***

NEWS BULLETIN. Breaking news just in that there has been a
shooting in a gay nightclub in Orlando, Florida. The man
who has been named by police as Mateen Omar, pledged
allegiance to so-called Islamic State. The nightclub is
situated on Orange Avenue and is well known in the
community for drawing a diverse crowd and for being a
place of solidarity and empowerment where people come
together… (*News report fades out.*)

***

AMINA. Things you need to know about me. My name's
Amina.

HELEN. My name's Helen.

AMINA. And if I had survived the Orlando shootings, then
today I would have graduated from Valencia College with a
major in Political Science.

HELEN. I live on Avalon Boulevard with my husband,
Carlton…

BETTY. My name's Betty and tomorrow, on my eighty-sixth
birthday, I am getting married.

HELEN. …and my daughter Jessica… and her girlfriend,
Sophie.

BETTY. Her name's Frankie. She's 'a younger woman' – sixty-
six. She likes tap-dancing and has a beautiful body and she

thinks I make the meanest cheese grills in the whole of
Memphis Tennessee. (*Smiles*.)

AMINA. I'd have interned at the UN, got a job at the Senate
and then the White House. After fifteen years at the White
House, I'd have gone to Pakistan to fight for women's rights
and to meet my family for the first time. On my return to
Florida I'd announce my intention to run. I'd have won by a
landslide. My name's Amina Hunzai and if I had survived
the June 12 shootings, my mom would tell me, on the night
of my inauguration, that my brother was living in Detroit…
that he was working in real estate… that he was married with
two girls – Salma and Amina… twins. If I had survived the
June 12 shootings, then I would write them. His girls, my
nieces. I would write them daily, on the Presidential
letterhead, and I would say… be you… keep on being you.

FUCKING FEMINISTS

Rose Lewenstein

[—] at the start of a line indicates a new voice

[—] mid-sentence indicates a change in thought

[—] at the end of a line indicates being cut off

[—] followed by a blank line indicates a marked silence

Written for an all-female cast of roughly five actors.

Unless explicitly referring to one another, characters address the audience.

Set: a chair.

— This is what a feminist looks like.

— This is what a feminist looks like.

— No. This is what a feminist looks like.

—

— Anyone or anything can be a feminist.

— A she, a he, a they —

— This chair, for example, could be a feminist.

— This chair has feminist qualities.

— It's a strong chair.

— A good role model for other chairs.

— This Chair Can.

— It is what it is.

— An inanimate object.

— This chair has been built by a person.

— Or assembled in a factory.

— Painted by a person.

— Or sprayed by some sort of machine.

— Someone, somewhere, designed this chair.

— A she, a he, a they —

— And if, for example, the person who designed, built, and/or painted this chair had branded it with, for example, the word Cunt —

— Does anyone here have a problem with the word Cunt?

— Perhaps the chair would like to reclaim the word Cunt.

— No doubt the chair has been in contact with many cunts.

— Perhaps the chair has been called a Cunt and thrown across the room.

— Perhaps its leg fell off.

— Perhaps someone fixed it with wood glue.

— And now it's fine.

—

—

—

— It is a very fine-looking chair.

— I'm sorry, did the chair ask for your opinion?

— I was paying it a compliment.

— The chair didn't ask for your opinion.

— The chair is an inanimate object and is therefore incapable of asking for an opinion.

— A person can choose whether or not to objectify herself or himself or themself but this chair has no choice.

—

— Fine. It's an ugly chair anyway.

—

— Useful but ugly.

— Functional.

— This chair was not built for the male gaze.

— Does that make it a feminist chair?

— I typed hashtag Feminism into Twitter and the first post I saw said: Feminism Is The Desperate Try Of Ugly Women To Become Attractive To Men.

— And yet there are men in this audience and they are looking at this chair.

— They see it as an object.

— Because it is an object.

— But they don't want to fuck the chair.

— Or maybe they do.

— Does anyone here want to fuck this chair?

—

— To someone, somewhere, this chair is a thing of beauty.

— A thing. Exactly.

— Ugliness is in the eye of the beholder.

— There's nothing wrong with Ugly.

— The world needs Ugly, otherwise Beauty doesn't exist.

— Just like Heaven wouldn't exist without Hell.

— Just like Heaven and Hell mean different things to different people.

— Burn all the ugly chairs.

—

— As a feminist, I have the right to burn a chair if I want to.

— As a feminist, I have the right to burn the hairs off my legs and underarms and upper lip and bikini line with laser treatment. If I want to.

— As a feminist, I have the right to let my hair grow.

— And as a feminist, I have the right to find body hair on other women repulsive.

— That's not very feminist of you.

— Feminism is not about body hair.

— Feminism is sometimes about body hair.

— Feminism is about choice. The right to choose.

— I have the right to choose how I define feminism.

— I have the right to choose whether or not I want to shave my legs.

— The right to choose whether or not I want to vote.

— The fact that a woman threw herself under a horse does not mean that I am obliged to vote.

— I can choose whether or not I want to conform to unrealistic beauty ideals perpetuated by the media.

— I can airbrush myself if I want to.

— I can get plastic surgery.

— I can completely change both my appearance and my personality. If I want to.

— Botox is very good these days.

— So is education. If you can afford it.

— Botox and education are both available to women.

— You can take out a loan for either.

— If the technician is good then you should still be able to move your forehead. Like this.

— If the university is good then you might get a job.

— If you get a job then you probably won't be paid as much as your male colleagues.

— If you have nice smooth skin then you may have more luck finding a partner.

— It's a tough choice.

— Botox is so good these days that at a certain age it's almost more of a statement not to have needles in your face than it is to go au naturel.

— It's like brushing your teeth. You have the right to choose not to, but why wouldn't you?

—

— Strike that.

— Botox is not the same as actual surgery. It's not the same as getting a boob job, for example.

— I have the right to pay to have my breasts augmented or filled with silicon if it makes me feel more confident about my appearance.

— If more women had boob jobs then more women would feel confident about their appearance. In theory.

— If no women had boob jobs then less women would want boob jobs.

— Anyone or anything can be a feminist. It doesn't matter whether your boobs are real or fake.

— It doesn't matter whether or not you are educated.

— But it helps.

— Breast enhancement or education?

— Feminism is about choice.

— The right to choose whether or not you want to vote.

— The right to choose whether or not you want labiaplasty.

— You have a choice. Unlike this chair.

— But the chair isn't influenced by the media.

— It's not even influenced by the people who sit on it.

— This chair will not hold a grudge if you, say, stand on it to change a light bulb.

— How many feminists does it take to change a light bulb?

— One. I think.

— Ten. One to change the light bulb and nine to blog about how empowering it was.

—

— I read it online.

— Why nine bloggers?

— I don't know, I read it online.

—

— Isn't it great how we can all laugh about this?

— Isn't it great how comfortable we all are with ourselves and with laughing at ourselves?

— It is really great.

— I'm talking about everyone, by the way. Not just feminists.

— I'm laughing on the outside but I'm screaming on the inside.

— Isn't it great that you can say that so openly?

— Yes, it is really great, I feel really great about it.

— It's very difficult to feel truly comfortable with yourself unless you are very drunk or very high or it's very dark.

— She's talking about everyone, by the way. Not just feminists.

— If it's dark enough then you can't see the wrinkles.

— If it's dark enough then you don't even need Botox.

— I like to sleep with the light on.

— She changes the bulb herself.

— No one blogs about it, she just changes it.

— I have dreams in which I'm buried alive.

— In some countries, women are buried alive as punishment.

— In this country, women were burned at the stake as punishment.

— And now they can vote.

— Isn't that fantastic?

— I have dreams in which I'm gang-banged by like twenty men and then I wake up and I'm actually having an orgasm. That's not very feminist of me, is it.

— No.

— Well.

— Maybe.

— I don't know.

— Feminism is about choice.

— Is it?

— You can't choose your dreams.

— You can't choose your fantasies.

— You can choose whether or not to objectify yourself.

— Unlike this chair.

— It can be difficult to draw a straight line between objectification and empowerment.

— If I write Cunt on the seat of this chair —

— If I then sit on that chair —

— If I have chosen to write the word Cunt and if I have chosen to sit on that chair —

— Is that objectification or is that empowerment?

— If I wear a low-cut top —

— If I let my date pay the bill —

— If I fuck a rich man for money —

— Is that objectification or empowerment?

— Please tick relevant box.

— It can be difficult to draw a straight line between feminism and feminism.

— There is a small hole in the glass ceiling for straight white privileged feminists to crawl through.

— Small being the operative word.

— Small straight white privileged feminists take up less space.

— Literally and figuratively.

— They don't exactly smash the ceiling. It's more like they tap at the glass until it cracks, forming a small hole through which they can crawl.

— Which is no small feat, don't get me wrong.

— It's painful cracking glass.

— Figuratively and literally.

— And once they're up there they call down to the others and they say: Anything Is Possible You Just Need To Believe In Yourself.

— And the rest of us look and we can just about see up their pencil skirts.

— Which is not very feminist of us.

— Smooth legs and expensive knickers.

— It's easy to get jealous when another feminist's floor is your ceiling.

— It's easy to get jealous of other feminists' expensive knickers, even if you have made a choice to only wear old period-stained pants.

— Feminism is about choice.

— Feminism is about all being in it together and at the same time recognising that none of us are equal.

— I typed Feminism Is into Google and it autocorrected to Feminism Is Cancer.

— Top-three search results for Feminism Is are Cancer, Bullshit and Wrong.

— So maybe this is bullshit and maybe we are wrong.

— All of us.

— Maybe I am a hypocrite for shaving my legs and wishing I had bigger boobs.

— Maybe I should just shut up and stop annoying people.

— I'm sorry, are we annoying you?

—

— Anything Is Possible You Just Need To Believe In Yourself.

— But what if you can't-slash-don't believe in yourself?

— Then, um, nothing is possible?

— I have the right to not believe in myself.

— Yes. I have the right to feel insecure about both my appearance and my personality.

— I have the right to be terrified of walking alone late at night in case I get raped and at the same time I have the right to think about sucking twenty cocks if it helps me to come.

— Anyone or anything has that right.

— A he, a she, a they —

— My boyfriend watches porn sometimes but he identifies as a feminist.

— My boyfriend won't do any housework but he also identifies as a feminist.

— People are complex, aren't they?

— My girlfriend says that just because she is a lesbian it doesn't mean she has to identify as a feminist.

— I don't have a boyfriend or a girlfriend because I find it easier to focus on Believing In Myself when I am single.

— Sometimes it's easier to just Shut Up And Get On With It.

— I typed hashtag Feminism into Twitter and the next post I saw said: Feminism Is The Fear And Anger That A Woman, Somewhere, Someplace, Is Happily Leading A Normal Life.

— And here we all are.

—

—

—

— I'm going to write Cunt on this chair.

—

— No one had a problem with the word Cunt, did they?

—

— Now I'm going to sit on it.

—

—

—

— I can't decide.

—

— I can't decide whether this is objectification or empowerment or neither.

— Sometimes a chair is just a chair.

— Sometimes a feminist is just a feminist.

— You can't always tell who's a feminist, even if they're wearing a T-shirt that says This Is What A Feminist Looks Like.

— No. Because it's about choice.

— It's about all being in it together and at the same time recognising that none of us are equal.

— Is it?

— Yes.

— Well.

— Maybe.

— I don't know.

—

—

—

—

—

— You should smile more.

— You should laugh. It's only a joke. This. We're only joking.

— It's just words.

—

—

—

— Look. The chair has reclaimed the word Cunt.

— Well, well-behaved chairs rarely make history.

   End.

TITUBA

Winsome Pinnock

Character

TITUBA

This is a one-woman show about Tituba Indian, an enslaved woman who played a central role in the Salem Village Witch Trials of 1692.

We discover TITUBA *sitting on stage, a rather demure character, a shawl about her wearing a mob cap.*

(1)

There was no dancing. No dancing, no drinking of blood. No black devil demanded our naked bodies for him to suckle on. There was no flying. I wish there had been flying. I would have taken flight long before the madness started. See Tituba skim the dark sky, Salem Village a speck of dirt in the wilderness; see her leap across stars, aflame with the power of the moon; but no, all there was on that winter night in Boston was a ragtag gathering of little girls – Betty the Reverend's daughter, Anne, the Putnams' girl, Mercy Lewis and Abigail Williams. The Reverend Parris was gone to fight another war with his church committee who tell him they will not deed him the church house.

(Somerset accent.) Prepostorous! The covenant not yet sealed, and you ask us to sign away the parsonage? If we deed you that house where will the next Reverend reside? And the next? Salem Village will have sold its soul to the lowest bid for the sake of one man's pecuniary gluttony. No, we'll not comply with yer. The church represents the body of this community, this parsonage its soul. And what is a body that has no soul?

Parris won't listen. I know him – he will fight until that house is given over to him, given over in perpetuity for him to pass to his children, his grandchildren and so on and so forth, forever and ever Amen. *(Slight pause.)* With Parris at the meeting house the parsonage is at rest, so his wife Elizabeth takes herself early to bed, while Betty and I are alone and free. But not for long. For when the Reverend is away the other girls hot-foot over to see us, begging me for stories and Indian cakes.

'What stories do I have for you?'

Tell us about the hairy Kenaima spirits that hide their evil intentions by taking the shape of birds or horses. Tell us how they get inside people and rip them apart from inside. Tell us how you swung naked through the trees. Show us how to shoot a bow and arrow.

'Bow and arrow? Abigail Williams. What do I know about such things?'

If you'll not tell us then we shall be the Indians ourselves. Look at me, I am an Indian! Watch me shoot my arrow, kerchow! (Feigns an exploding head.) Blood everywhere. Did you see her head explode?' (Hollers and runs about like an 'Indian'.)

'There will be no blood or exploding heads. You will play like good children.'

(Abigail hollers like an Indian.)

'You will get me into trouble, Abigail Williams.'

(Abigail hollers.)

Who's to stop us? We'll play if we want to. Why should we take orders from a slave woman?

She is not a slave. Betty is almost in tears. As usual, Abigail wants a fight, but I am exhausted from the day's work and have no strength for it.

'Be good, girls. Or I will tell the Reverend when he returns.'

The mention of his name is enough to bring them to order. The war gives way to demure Bible lessons and darning. And that is how we pass the time, until someone – I don't remember who – it could have been any one of those children – Abigail, Betty, Mercy or Ann – says *Let's tell each other's fortunes*. The Reverend would forbid it, but it is an innocent game, and they have been so good.

'All right. Betty, fetch the eggs. And a glass.'

This is how the story begins: with the cracking of an egg to read the future from the shape of its yolk. Mercy goes first, pours the egg into the glass. We wait to see what shape it will take.'

It's a heart, says Abigail.

You will have a husband, Mercy.

The promise of a husband comforts an eleven-year-old servant girl whose backside is raw with whipping for a thousand misdemeanours. Because I already have a man in John the Indian, Betty takes my turn. She holds the egg in her hand, feeling its coolness. She is only nine, but dreams of a husband to rescue her from the Reverend who is the most demanding of fathers.

Go on, Betty. Crack it.

Abigail prods Betty's shoulder leaving a yellow spot where her finger touches. Betty doesn't move. She is afraid of the future. An icy wind blows onto the porch and we are suddenly aware of the wilderness that surrounds us. From deep within it the call of some animal, like a muffled scream. We huddle closer together.

(Whispers.) It's the Indians. We can't see them, but they're watching us. Everywhere we go. Everything we do. They're waiting. So, help me God, Betty, they'll shoot an arrow straight into your head, if you don't get a move on and crack that egg.

Abigail shoves Betty's arm. The egg smashes on the rim and slides into the glass, but the yolk does nothing, floats in its waters until Abigail pricks it with a darning pin. We all watch as a terrible future takes shape. Nobody moves, nobody speaks, until Abigail says the unsayable.

It's a coffin. Betty's going to die. You're going to die, Betty.

Betty's face contorts with a pain that I feel as though she was from my own womb. She bites her lip, but I, who have read her face since the day she was born, feel her terror. 'No, my Betty will not die.' And then it comes, the voice.

But we're all going to die, Tituba.

(Frightened.) The Reverend? Returned already? I can tell from his sunken eyes, his pale face that the meeting has not gone his way.

Is this what you do the minute I turn my back? Does my absence signify your freedom from the word of God? Does it not occur to you that God's eyes are upon you at all times? You can climb the tallest tree, burrow underground, but God will find you. As Abel's blood called out from the dirt he was buried under, I will find you out.

It was just a game, Reverend Parris, a silly game of fortunes.

Games, is it? What does the Bible say of games? The Bible says that anyone who practises divination or tells fortunes, whoever does these things is an abomination to the Lord. And those who are an abomination to the Lord are thrown into the lake of fire, there to burn eternally alongside the beast himself, a devil so gnarled and blackened with sin.

(*Pause.*)

Sometimes in church on a Sunday when the Reverend preaches his sermon Ann Putnam drops her prayer book and indicates that I am to fetch it. She meets me there on the ground and grabs my hand when I return her the book, digs her nails into my palms to staunch a fit of giggles. There follows a frenzy of popping prayer books and the girls and I hold on to each other, cowering under the pews.

And now, with the Reverend glaring at us, his face so purple he could be that black beast himself. I have a sudden desire to laugh. A tremor in the pit of my stomach rises up through my belly and chest, passes my throat, and into my mouth. Betty trembles beside me and I know that she wants to laugh too. The trembling sparks across the circle of girls. It has taken fire. Abigail sneezes. The Reverend turns around sharp to look at her, not knowing, as we do, that the sneeze is a cover for a giggling girl. This makes Mercy burst out laughing. The Reverend's head spins like an owl's. We are all laughing. It is a bonfire of laughter. The Reverend cannot believe what he sees.

Cease. Tituba, I command you to stop.

But I can't. (*Laughs.*)

Stop-stop I say!

Then he says the one thing that will put an end to it:

Betty, fetch me the whip.

The girls remain still. Fear consumes Betty's face. She does not move. She has seen me beaten before.

Why does he beat you so? What have you done wrong?

It is not a punishment. It is to make me a slave.

What is a slave?

A slave is a half-human creature

Like a ghost?

A ghost is free. I am not a ghost.

I'll burn that whip he hits you again. I mean it. He'll not touch you again, Tituba

The woman who birthed her floats through the house like a phantom so I am the only mother she has known. In secret I teach her words from the old life.

'Tadewi... wind'

Tadewi

'Amitola... rainbow'

Amitola

You should have heard her holler the first time she saw herself in a mirror: who is this white imposter-baby? She imagines herself brown like me; spits and scratches at the glass to rid herself of her rival.

The whip, Betty!

Betty doesn't hear him. I will her to move her feet. Do what he says, Betty, or it will be bad for all of us.

Betty, do you hear me? She doesn't answer

No Betty, no. This is not the moment. Fetch him the whip. But she doesn't hear my thoughts. And then something remarkable happens. Betty's hands fly up over her head. She is on her toes as though pulled up by some force.

I cannot move. I cannot move!

Stop this, child. And do as I say.

I want to, but something holds me!

No, Betty, no. This is no time for games.

The Reverend goes to her, takes hold of her shoulders and she is all legs and arms, kicking and raining blows down on him.

Betty, stop this.

I cannot. I have lost the use of my body! Somebody help me!

No, Betty, no.

He drops her onto the ground where she kicks and flails like a dog chasing its tail.

Where have you gone? All is dark. I cannot see! I cannot see! Give me back my eyes. Mercy, flails with her hands in front of her

Ann has fallen to the ground, her body strange and twisted about.

I see, says Abigail. *I see a demon sitting on your shoulder, Reverend Parris. It is black and hairy and small as a bird. Your head is open and it pecks at your brains. Can't you feel it?*

Parris turns to face me.

Tituba. What in God's name have you done?

And so it begins.

(2)

My first mistress, Mrs Pearsehouse, owned a plantation in Barbados. Because I am Indian I work in the house and not in the fields with the Africans. They toil from sunset to sunrise cutting cane. They do not look at each other when they are in the fields. Sometimes they sing in their different languages. All the different songs coming together in one. Mrs Pearsehouse likes to hear that singing. She says it shows how happy they are, but the singing stirs a longing and an empty sadness inside me.

Mrs Pearsehouse spends her days receiving visitors like Mrs Cooper for whom I prepare wine made from cassava. They tell me it is delicious and I wonder what they would say if they knew that I make it like we used to in the old life: chew the cassava, spit the juice and leave it to ferment.

Mrs Pearsehouse keeps me by her side like a shadow. She puts me in a dress that is identical to hers, although hers is made of embroidered silk and mine of coarse linen. We are strange twins.

She never goes out onto the plantation, leaving that to her son. She does not like to see the Africans beaten, although she says it is the only way to make them work. She stays in the house to protect her skin and teaches me the English customs so that she can entertain as though she had never left home. It amuses her to show me off to Mrs Cooper who compliments Elizabeth on the excellent job she has done with me.

If you could only hear her speak, but did not see her face you would think she was as white as this bone-china teacup. Tell me, Tituba, do you remember your old life at all?

'I don't remember the old ways and I don't want to remember them. What? Go back to running through the jungle with a bow and arrow? I am grateful, Mrs Pearsehouse. Yes, I thank God for the sailors who lured us onto their ship with the promise of trading our shells for furs and magic powders. If I had understood God's plan for me I would not have put up such a furious fight and jumped overboard into the freezing seas. When I swam for my life I was not to know that I was swimming away from my own salvation. How would I have known my value if I hadn't been made to stand, manacled in the auction house and have men prod my cheek, look into my mouth, examine my flank, my rump, made me walk up and down before them naked; if I hadn't seen two – no three, no four – men haggling over me?

Would you give me ten? Thank you, sir. Ten-dollar bidder now ten now ten. Higgidy diggidum diggidum higgidy ten-dollar bidder. Give me twelve dollar thank you. Twelve-dollar bidder now twelve now twelve. Twelve-dollar bidder diggidum diggidum. Twelve-dollar bidder. Sold right there for twelve dollars to Samuel Pearsehouse.

'And what a man Samuel Pearsehouse is. Although I am a child, he honours me by coming to my bed at night. He tells me that, until God sees fit to send him a decent bride, I must serve him in wifely duties. Takes possession and spurts his blessed seed into me. I am grateful that the children I bear are sold for profit as pets to the offspring of other planters. I do not cry when they are taken from me. Though slaves are human in form, they do not feel, they do not cry for their lost children at night. Just as we do not tire when you work us to death, we do not beat ourselves about in a rage of grief so that the physical hurt obliterates the pain in our hearts. Thank you, Mrs Pearsehouse for making me a happy slave.'

Mrs Pearsehouse and Mrs Cooper stare at me. The grandfather clock tries to change the subject by chiming the hour. The women can't accuse me of mocking them because they would have to admit that I had a mind capable of doing so. When Mrs Cooper has gone Mrs Pearsehouse sends me to fetch the whip. She undoes my dress as though she is *my* body servant and orders me to curtsy before I offer her my back.

(3)

News of the bewitched girls has raced across Salem. Betty and Abigail sit about the house neither dead or alive, their eyes staring into a world the rest of us cannot see. The Reverend seeks but cannot find a cause for their illness. He sends for Dr Griggs who makes his examination. He tries to prise them out of their contorted poses, but they cannot be untangled. He lifts their eyelids and talks to them to see if they can hear him. As he listens to Betty's heart she starts to speak: spits out a strange language.

(*Very fast.*) *Tadewtaimatehyaunataimatadewa*
Tadewtaimatehyaunataimatadewa

Is she speaking in tongues? What does it mean? What is she saying, Dr Griggs?

Tadewtaimatehyaunataimatadewa
Tadewtaimatehyaunataimatadewa

Griggs moves away, alarmed.

This sickness is not of the body, sir, but has some otherworldly cause. Reverend, you are more trained in the healing of such ailments than I. I cannot help you.

*Tadewtaimatehyaunataimatadewamitola
Tadewtaimatehyaunataimatadewamitola*

What are you saying, Betty? Are these words from God or the devil? Which is it?

As I listen I realise that I know those words. She speaks fast-very-fast, but I can still make them out. Tadewi… wind; amitola… rainbow. Betty remembers. She remembers the words I taught her as a baby. She has not forgotten. They are just words, Reverend Parris, innocent words. He doesn't hear me.

Tell me, child. Who has bewitched you? You will not be punished for this game if you tell me the truth

The babble subsides. Betty is exhausted. As she falls asleep again, Abigail comes to life.

Tell me, child. Who has bewitched you?

Abigail stands.

Abigail has lived with her uncle, the Reverend Parris for the past four years. She is an orphan whose parents were killed during an Indian raid. She never speaks of what she saw, but wakes shouting in the night. When I go to her she is a ball of fear hiding in the corner of the room.

There's men out there. I heard footsteps, their hollerin', saw their shadows pass across the window. They've come for me. They'll cut my head off and put it on a stick. Please don't let them take me.

I look outside, tell her there is nothing there, that I will watch until she goes to sleep. She hides her fits of anger from the Reverend but inflicts them on me. Hurls Elizabeth's best dish to the ground.

Tituba did it. I saw her. She's hate and spite in her, that slave woman

What can I say? Who will listen? I too have witnessed much, we have that in common. She is not a slave, but neither is she free.

Tell me, child. Who has bewitched you?

Abigail stands and walks towards me

(4)

The Reverend Parris wants me to relieve his cursed household by confessing that I am to blame. 'Confess, you nigger-heathen.' Nigger? Heathen? Me, Tituba in whom all trace of what I once was has been erased? As the whip burns my back I send my mind out of my body like a bird and I am back in the old life. I see my mother standing at the seashore where she waits every day for me to return.

She blows bubbles into the water, filling each with the whisper of my name, telling the river to carry them to the sea, which she hopes will find me. She performs the dance of the night dancers, willing its magic to keep me safe.

(TITUBA *performs her mother's dance. As the dance ends she howls her mother's pain at her loss*.)

When I return to my body the Reverend Parris swings the leather and lashes the air, splitting my soul into three pieces. The first hovers over his shoulder and I see myself as he sees me, my back soggy with blood, but still he lashes out, his muscles pulsing. A shadow on the wall shows us as a single furious creature. The second counts each thrash of the whip. The slave code permits seventy-five lashes, and he passed that minutes ago. Ninety-nine... You will confess... Thrash! it was you bewitched the children... Thrash-thrash-thrash!... The third piece recites my worth in my mind. I'm bid fifty-dollar bidder now fifty now would you give me hundred? Thank you sir. Hundred-dollar bidder now hundred now hundred now hundred. I count the lashes... hundred and sixty. Hundred dollar dollar now hundred now hundred. Hundred and seventy... Thrash!... hundred dollar dollar now hundred now hundred... Hundred and eighty-eight... Thrash! Hundred dollar dollar now hundred

now hundred. Two hundred... Thrash! Sold to the Reverend
Parris for two hundred lashes. (*Barely able to speak after the
whipping*.) I confess. I am a witch. I confess it.

(5)

John weeps as he tends to my back.

Haven't you been whipped before, John?

Not like this. I should have protected you.

'How could you? They would kill you.'

I should die fighting for you.

'They are afraid of us, John. They know we have been done a
terrible wrong and they are afraid that we will take our
revenge.'

And one day we will.

I do not want him to look at me. Tadewi... Amitola... He blows
on my back. His breath is warm then cool. Tadewi... Amitola...
He strokes and kisses my hand. I cannot bear his touch. It is a
relief when he is sent to fetch wood and I am left alone. I kick
off the rags. I will not wear their clothes any more. The whip
shredded my disguise to reveal the black skin underneath. The
blood continues to seep out of me. I am too weak to move. I
sink into the earth. Take me. Bury me under the dirt. Take me
home.

(6)

I open my eyes to a strange sight: the room is full of bubbles.
They float through the air and make a curious music. I pop one
with my fingers. As it pops it releases a sound. My mother's
voice. I pop another and another. Her voices fill the room. She
chants my name, calls me back to her. Not the name given me
by the traders, but the name she gave me; my real name. They
cannot take my name. I have kept it locked away inside me. Not
even John knows my name. But now I unleash it into the room.
I say it over and over again, send its power into my wounds and

a rapid healing ensues: blood congeals, scars harden, clamping like armour onto my back. I say it louder so that it fills the space like a battle cry. I am myself again. I am no longer your Tituba. I have slipped Tituba off like a chrysalis. I watch her as she lies on the pallet. Look at her a weakened, empty husk. Rest now, Tituba. I will breathe new life into you. I will make the Reverend pay for what he has done to you. I will make them all pay for my mother's grief.

You destroyed my mother and now I will destroy yours.

(7)

A crowd follows Constable Herrick who makes his way to the Parris residence, charged with the arrest of Tituba Indian. The crowd grows bigger as Herrick leads me to the meeting house, already packed with spectators. I am set before Mr Hale, my confessor, who towers above me. The stricken girls, Ann, Betty, Mercy and Abigail are in the charge of the elders. The only person who will not look at Tituba is the Reverend Parris. He is willing me to do as he bids. His fate lies in my hands but, because he owns me, he has nothing to fear. I have a part to play and I play it well, darting looks around the court like a frightened animal. To those gathered in the meeting house I appear childlike and inferior of mind.

Hale stands and I shiver as I look up at him, make myself as small as he is tall.

Titibe, what evil spirit do you have familiarity with?

Say none, I tell myself. I must draw them in slowly.

'None.'

The Reverend's hands are shaking. He presses them on his lap and examines a speck of blood on his finger.

Why do you hurt these children?

I do not hurt them.

Who is it then?

'The Devil for ought I know.'

Hale's eyes widen in surpise.

Did you never see the Devil?

He is an expert in the extracting of confessions. I take
advantage of his conceit.

'The Devil came to me and bid me serve him.'

Hale thinks he is onto something. He is not to know that I am
holding the reins in one hand and a whip in the other. With each
movement I send him in the desired direction. He takes the bit.

Who have you seen?

'Two women sometimes hurt the children.'

Who were they?

Now, Tituba, now. You have the whip in your hand. You are the
auctioneer. Pick a name, any name. Just as you were ripped at
random from your mother's arms and from the life that you
knew, now you will tear their lives apart. I look around the court.
Silence. They are waiting for me to speak. I name the names.

'Goody Osborne and Sarah Good.'

Hale turns to the gathering, triumphant. He believes you. He
believes you. Abigail darts a look at me. A moment passes as
she realises that she can no longer punish me by accusation: I
am her mistress now. She breaks free of the elders and assumes
her crude postures. The other girls follow suit. The court reacts:
the spirit has descended on the court and is manipulating the
girls like puppets. Abigail, Betty, Mercy and Ann know that,
unless they do what I want them to, they will be lashed to near
death by my confession. One by one they corroborate my story
and start to cry out:

***I seen Martha Corey with the Devil. I seen Dorcas Good with
the Devil.***

The Reverend Parris is shaking as though he too is possessed.
He expected me to confess, but did not reckon that I would
name names. Do not worry, Reverend. I will not name you.
There is no need: in time you will be annihalated by your own
wickedness.

I seen Rebecca Nurse with the Devil. I seen Rachel Clinton with the Devil.

Bridget Bishop, John Lee, Sara Cloyce. Father against son, brother against sister. I could not have predicted this outcome.

I seen Sarah Wilds with the Devil...

Perhaps I really am a witch. Certainly, I can see the future: farms go untended, cows and sheep perish, money lost. Twenty-four men, women and babies killed. The suffering passed down for generations. Such is my power.

I seen Mary Easty with the Devil. I seen George Burroughs with the Devil...

The Reverend Parris will visit me in prison. He will sweet-talk me to name the names of those on the church committee who oppose him. He will make promises he cannot keep, leave Tituba to rot in jail before she disappears from history. Oh yes, things will return to normal in time. I will know my place once more. But for the moment Tituba is free and Salem is in chains.

I seen Nehemiah Abbot with the Devil. I seen Margaret Hawkes with the Devil.

Fly, Tituba, fly! Mother against daughter, wife against husband and on and on. The madness consumes them.

(*Pause.*)

I stand at the back of the court and watch Salem destroy itself.

Ends.

THE ROAD TO HUNTSVILLE

Stephanie Ridings

Character

STEPH

A solo show for a female performer.

The screen and images should be as integral to the text as the person performing it. If used, they should be individual to each performer and production.

Nothing and everything is real.

1 – The Beginning

You know when you're a little kid and they tell you the bogeyman is going to come and get you and you're supposed to feel scared? Well I always had a fantasy that the bogeyman came all dressed in black, black leather and he was riding on this big black stallion and he comes to my bedroom window, he comes to get me and I jump on the horse with him and I wrap my arms round his waist and I get under his cape and we fly away.

Beat.

These are not my words they are the words of an American woman in her early fifties, with wavy brown hair and bright-red lips.

Let's call her Blanche.

Blanche is in love with a serial killer, who raped and murdered five students. She smiles and flirts with the camera as she explains she instantly felt attracted to him. He made her feel like a real woman. He's a person and her feelings are based on him as a person.

Image of 'Blanche'. Her face is covered up.

I'm tempted to tell you her real name and show you a proper picture but the documentary she is being interviewed for is exploiting her enough already. If you are interested put 'Serial Killer Groupies' into YouTube. Her surname matches England's capital.

A younger woman now, mid-twenties long straight dark hair. Let's call her Terri, with an I. Terri with an I was in love with a serial killer, he was charged with thirteen counts of murder and eleven of rape – that they could prove. Terri looks awkward as she describes him as hot, really hot, his eyes, his face his hair. She fell in love with him through his letters. They were pen pals.

Now there are hundreds of Blanches and Terries when you start to look and like me you may be thinking they're spinsters, with cats, who rarely leave the house – unless posting a letter to an inmate – but no, there are Danielles too.

Danielle Steel Wikipedia page.

I'm not sure how familiar you are with the literary works of Danielle Steel.

The fourth best-selling author of all time, according to Wikipedia.

Also, according to Wikipedia, two of her five marriages were to convicts. She met both men whilst they were incarcerated. One was actually released on parole whilst they were dating and whilst he was out he raped a woman. Once back inside she married him in the prison canteen.

So let's confirm that little bit of information. Danielle Steel married a man who raped a woman whilst they were together.

Pause.

Voice-over of women and images of prisoners.

'I've always had a thing for bad boys.'

'I wanted to know everything about him. I wanted to know if he did what he really did.'

'You just wanna break down the glass and get 'em out.'

'It was a beautiful courtship and I don't think we get to be courted any more.'

'I know that he killed a lot of people but I didn't really care about that.'

'Some people are just supposed to be together whether there's a cage or lawman between you.'

'People fall in love all over the world and for all different reasons. I just happened to fall in love with a man on death row.'

These women are writers, journalists, lawyers, teachers, nurses, civil servants, mothers, wives. They come from a range of social backgrounds, do a range of jobs, are a range of ages and are scattered across the world.

They're not serious though are they. They can't believe any of it is real. How can you find your soulmate through letters or bulletproof glass? Surely they're just projecting a fantasy onto the men. And these men, these are some of society's worst. Murderers, rapists, necrophiles, serial killers, psychopaths, master manipulators. Surely they just want the women for the money they send and perhaps the odd risqué photo to trade with the other inmates.

I only do a little digging into this subject and I'm hooked and realise I could write a play about this.

So I order a book called *Women Who Love Men Who Kill*, and whilst I wait for it to arrive I get stuck into every documentary I can find.

Images on screen accompany following text:

'*Inside Death Row with Trevor McDonald.*'

A few Louis Theroux bits.

Lots by Werner Herzog.

'*Life and Death Row*' – via the BBC.

'*The Final Twenty-Four Hours.*'

'*Serial Killer Groupies.*'

'*Taboo: Love On Death Row.*'

'*The Last 40 Miles.*'

'*Married Behind Bars.*'

'*Death Row Dates.*'

'*Love Behind Bars.*'

Erm no can't remember that one.

'*Fourteen Days in May.*'

'*At the Death House Door.*'

I watch them all, over and over in case I miss anything, which may be super important.

Occasionally I throw in a cat GIF just to keep things light.

Show cat GIF.

I watch these documentaries over and over and tell myself it's research, even though I've already watched them, studied them and made comprehensive notes. I study them again and make new notes because present me is always to be trusted over past me.

Each night the other half, Stompy – Stompy as he always stomps off whenever we row – Stompy comes home from work and he starts making dinner whilst I lean up against the kitchen door and regale him with what facts I uncovered that day.

Facts appear on screen as she lists them.

Most, if not all executions are carried out by lethal injection. This was a three-drug system but due to shortage it is now a one-drug system.

There is a higher percentage of poor, black and ethnic-minority inmates in prison and on death row.

You're likely to spend an average of fifteen years waiting to be executed.

Texas is only the third largest death row in the USA but it executes the most people.

On Texas death row you spend nearly twenty-three hours a day locked up.

And that's in solitary confinement and that's every day.

Beat.

Stompy is worried I'm getting in too deep, becoming too obsessed again. I remind him I'm a very thorough researcher. And distract him with this.

Show cat GIF.

I am still awaiting the arrival of the book *Women Who Love Men Who Kill*. So I decide to leave death row procedures alone and instead have a look at the men available for pen palling.

I settle on writeaprisoner.com.

Show website page.

There are nine thousand, two hundred and thirty-six live ads from prisoners on this website alone and that's before you even get to Met Whilst Incarcerated, Prison Talk, Meet an Inmate, Human Writes, Friendship Beyond the Wall, Prison Inmates, Minutes Before Six, and so on.

Nine thousand, two hundred and thirty-six seems quite an overwhelming number of profiles so I select men. I select Texas. I select death row.

It's at this stage of the research I decide to throw caution to the wind and leave astrological sign unspecified.

See results and flick through them.

Twenty-nine results.

Their faces and profiles stare at me.

Posing in their prison regulation. What they assume is a warm, welcoming smile.

They show their muscles. Their tats. Their humanity.

With the exception of Tomas, who looks like the psychopath he probably is.

Flick through each profile.

Christopher is 'excited by the chance of an encounter with a complete stranger'.

Randy is a 'Twelve-and-a-half and is unlike any other brother'. A twelve-and-a-half what? That really needs to be clearer, Randy.

Troy wants a shot.

Franklin wants a photo – I bet he bloody does.

Douglas is innocent.

John is just a small puppy, hoping someone will hear him and throw him a bone.

Let's have a little look at what John the small puppy is on death row for.

John's TDCJ – Texas Department of Criminal Justice – page.

He shot and killed a twenty-one-year-old white woman and twenty-three-year-old white male. And I can tell you that was his ex-girlfriend and her brother. John is just hoping to find a non-judgemental pen pal.

Beat.

I don't get it.

I look at these men and I read their profiles and I don't find anything about them attractive. They sound like they're the victims and of course the majority of them are innocent, but not one profile would send me reaching for a pen and paper.

I get this uneasy feeling that I'm not taking this subject matter seriously enough.

People are dying. State-sanctioned homicide.

I look at this picture.

Show Texas execution chamber.

This is the execution chamber in Texas.

I look at this picture and I see a room painted green and wonder why they chose that particular colour.

I look up the word sociopath. I do a Facebook quiz. I am satisfied I'm not a sociopath.

Besides, if I find this funny then I can't be can I? Right? Right?

Show cat GIF.

Finally, *Women Who Love Men Who Kill* arrives. I get stuck in straight away. I make notes but it slows me down too much so I commit a crime against literature. I hate people who do this. I hate myself for doing it. But I get a highlighter and mark sections of text. I disgust myself.

Once I move past the horror of highlighting, I discover the following:

There is a term hybristophilia. This is when women are attracted to men who have committed extreme crimes. Also worth mentioning, women who have hybristophilia tend to masturbate after reading about these types of criminals.

Although the women may be from a range of backgrounds they generally share experience of abuse.

The women think they can rescue the men and want to share his spotlight.

A high percentage of women have had a Catholic upbringing and are in their thirties/forties.

Some are lost in the fantasy of the perfect boyfriend.

Fundamentally women are looking for an alpha male to protect and save them. Rapist-slash-killers are the ultimate alpha male.

'Fundamentally women are looking for an alpha male to protect and save them.'

What the fuck?

Puts book in the bin.

2 – Reaching Out / Sandy

I start hanging round online forums.

This one is my favourite.

See Met Whilst Incarcerated webpage.

Met Whilst Incarcerated.

I don't actually post anything myself, I just judge everyone who does.

Actually, whatever I think about the women who post here, they stick together and support each other. Women from all across the world, from all walks of life they've got each other's backs, they're part of something together.

I contemplate reaching out to someone through one of these forums. Hours of searching and wondering if making contact with someone is the right thing to do and I have found her. TexasRose3. Actual name Sandy Demouchette.

Show Sandy's Facebook page.

Sandy is a schoolteacher and in her spare time an anti-death-penalty campaigner. She also happens to have a brother currently housed on death row in Texas. I write her a message, I'm a writer doing research and all that business and send it before I have chance to change my mind.

She replies within the hour.

See Sandy's Facebook page.

I'm a bit disappointed as the majority of her email looks like a standard response that goes out to everyone. Stuff about the death penalty being a broken process. That it violates the constitutional ban against cruel and unusual punishment. Solitary confinement costs too much and exacerbates mental illness.

She points me in the direction of some pictures showing where her brother is housed.

Images of Texas death row.

They speak for themselves.

She encourages me to join the cause and wonders if I may like to correspond with her brother Jonny Demouchette.

I stop reading her email at this point. I'm heading into uncomfortable territory. This is getting a bit close isn't it? I mean it's all very well looking at stuff on the internet and making stories up about what you find but crashing into someone's life for the purposes of a better story? Does it make it more authentic? Would they say anything different to what is already out in the public domain? Shit! Should I even have contacted Sandy?

Beat.

I get her brother Jonny Demouchette up on the TDCJ website. Just to see what his crime was, and well having a look at him wouldn't hurt either.

STEPH *has a printout*.

He looks like a Hispanic James Dean.

'On 03/05/2001 in Jefferson, Demouchette murdered a thirty-nine-year-old Middle Eastern male convenience-store employee during an attempted robbery.'

So that's a burglary gone wrong?

At least he's not a rapist or a serial killer.

And he didn't murder his girlfriend or wife.

Surely this is just a moment of madness. One bad decision and now he's paying for it with his life. Any one of us could find ourselves making the wrong decision in the heat of the moment. I mean granted we wouldn't necessarily be making that wrong decision with a .38 caliber Smith & Wesson in our hands but… you get me?

3 – First Contact

Stompy and I live in one of those houses where the front door opens directly into the living room. I worried for ages if this would be okay as we have a one-eyed house cat.

Show image of cat.

And he doesn't go outside unaccompanied and what if he one day decided to make a break for freedom. To feel the wind in his fur, the concrete under his paws. Not that he would, he is perfectly content but you know.

So, anyway the front door right onto our living room, it's fine apart from when you're totally engrossed in something and someone creeps up the path to put something through the letter box and me and the cat shit ourselves in unison wondering if this is a home invasion but realising, it's just a letter.

Just a letter.

This isn't just a letter. This is the letter. As it lies on the mat untouched, unopened, I know this is Jonny's letter. I'm very good at detective-slash-research stuff. Some may even say stalking. Whatever, I'm good at it. But none of those skills are required for me to know it's from him as it says, 'Sender Jonny Demouchette' and the prison address on the envelope. A letter coming from death row sat on my mat.

I've touched something that has been on death row in Texas. I've touched something that Jonny has touched who lives on death row and has murdered someone.

For the next twenty minutes I dance round the table. Moving towards it. Moving away. The cat thinks it's a game, he likes to play Hide-and-Seek. I turn it into that and chase him and hide to reassure myself I'm not mental.

Each time I return the letter is still sat there. Lifeless. Harmless. Just a letter.

Tentatively opens letter.

White, thin paper.

Written with a typewriter.

I'm not sure if I imagine it but I'm sure the paper smells of institution.

'I hope this letter finds you in light and love.' – Christ, this doesn't bode well does it?

'Your letter was a joy to receive and a most welcome light in the greyness that is death row on the Polunsky unit here in Texas.

I'm so glad my sister passed my details onto you. Always the campaigner is sis! It's nice to know outside of these walls people haven't forgotten us though.

Your project sounds interesting. There are few guys back here who have married or have girlfriends who started off as pen pals. I've had a few pen pals but nothing romantic. All lovely women, who I love and have the deepest respect for. Some guys don't have any contact with the outside world apart from their lawyers. They have it the toughest. That's why people put out ads. It's really for friendship. To pass the long lonely hours we are all doing back here.'

4 – The Progression

And that's how it starts.

Letters going out to Livingston in Texas and coming back to Kenilworth in Warwickshire.

Months go by like this.

Me: I live in a town in middle England. It has lots of yummy mummies and competitive parenting. I'm like the diversity for the area as I'm northern.

Him: I'd love a picture of you for my wall.

Me: I have a one-eyed house cat. He has supervised visits into the garden, sometimes on a lead.

Him: I haven't seen the stars in years and years and years. And I miss the rain and really, really good food. Ribs, steak, a fine burger.

I'm originally from a seaside town called Blackpool. I've enclosed pictures of the Tower, piers and Pleasure Beach.

I'm on death row for killing a grocery store worker for forty-two dollars and a crate of beer. A stupid kid who made a mistake and is paying with his life.

I've been with my partner for twelve years, we're struggling a bit, I'm struggling a bit.

I remember not wanting to step into my cell, as if moving inside would be admitting this was it.

I've been having a bad week. I want to snap out of it but don't seem to be able to. I'm thinking of getting my medication upped. I'd rather hoped I'd be off it by now.

It breaks my heart my mum died with me in here. Her last image of me was in prison regs behind bullet-proof glass.

My brother has had his diagnosis through. It is Asperger's. We're hoping this will be a turning point.

I haven't felt the touch of another human being in fourteen years.

I feel I could tell you anything. You always seem to get it, get me.

5 – An Invitation

The Governor of Texas finally signs Jonny's death warrant. He has a date.

Everyone knew this day was coming. It's not a total surprise, out of the blue. Appeals can still be made.

There are all the problems with the drugs they use, to start with. It's been all over the news, have you seen it? So, it used to be a three-drug system and companies stopped supplying one of them as it's not ethical is it? And so now it's a one-drug system and there was this man in Oklahoma or was it Ohio, I can't remember, anyway it was taking him an hour to die and just as they were about to stop the execution he had a heart attack and died anyway. So yes, the lawyers think there are plenty of grounds to pursue a stay.

Jonny jokingly writes if ever I'm passing Texas it would be great for me to stop by and see him. His sister Sandy says something similar but there is no way I can go to Texas. Is there? The money for a start. And Texas. It's hardly round the corner is it. And where would I stay?

When Stompy gets home from work I casually mention Jonny has his execution date. Stompy has got himself in a right state over all this research business. I've even been sent to sleep in the spare room. The cat has joined me. Who said cats aren't loyal?

And anyway, it's Stompy's own fault, he shouldn't have gone looking at stuff that doesn't concern him. I don't go to his work and start opening his drawers and looking at his emails and files.

Reading a letter.

'I feel like we have been friends for many years and yet we hardly know each other. I have such strong love for you. You have awoken feelings in me, which have laid dormant for years. If I was a free man I'd marry you tomorrow, hell make that today. But I'm just a condemned man wondering if you'll marry me anyway?'

I know. I know I should have mentioned that letter but everything is such hard work with Stompy lately it makes me want to go to sleep. And as I explained, or tried to, it's just research. And Jonny's not serious. And even if I did marry him and I'm not actually going to, it would be for research and they're going to execute him so I'd no longer be married pretty quickly and is that marriage even legal over here?

You can imagine how that went down.

A man in a maximum-security prison four thousand miles away is hardly a threat.

He didn't see it that way and wanted to know what I had been writing to Jonny for him to say these things.

Maybe, just maybe Jonny wanted to say nice things and make me feel good about myself. Make me feel wanted, loved rather than nag about the dishes not being washed to his standard, or who has or hasn't put the rubbish out or washed clothes or been food shopping or washed the car or mowed the lawn or cleaned the bathroom or changed the cat litter.

I knew I was on rocky territory when I informed him Sandy had invited me over – Obviously I'm not completely stupid and didn't mention Jonny had also extended an invite.

The excessive banging around in the kitchen was enough to let me know his thoughts on the matter.

It wasn't like I was going to go but Sandy put me on Jonny's visitation list, just in case and said she might start the forms for

us to marry at the prison. I looked at where I might fly from and
how much it would cost and how long it would take. Sandy said
I could stay with her but if I was going to go I'd prefer a hotel
so she suggested a place. And I found myself looking at car hire
and driving in the States.

And that's what credit cards are for, isn't it?

Pause.

Several accusations get thrown backwards and forwards.

I feel ignored.

He feels I don't fancy him any more.

I feel we're stale.

He feels taken for granted.

I feel we're going round in circles.

He feels I need stronger antidepressants.

I feel he's overreacting.

He feels because I have a significant birthday coming up that
maybe I'm having a midlife crisis.

I feel that is really, really fucking rude.

Beat.

I book my flights, motel and car hire.

He grabs my arms tight so I can't move and inches from my
face says 'None of this is real. What the fuck are you doing?'

Punching you in the face in a minute if you don't take your
fucking hands off me.

Stompy tells me if I go that's us.

I don't understand why he is threatened by a research trip. It's a
research trip so I can make a piece of theatre and he is dealing
ultimatums out about the rest of our lives.

He means it, he really means it. If I love him, if our life together
means anything I'm not to go.

6 – Huntsville

Image of the Huntsville sign. STEPH *stands in front of it. When she moves she is in the picture in the same place.*

Huntsville, Walker County, Texas.

Let me show you round give you a feel for the place.

Montage of Huntsville.

The best way to describe it is that it feels like being on the set of *Back to the Future*. The first one, when Michael J Fox has gone back, and the clock still works.

I find myself hanging round the cultural quarter quite a bit which 12th Street runs through. At the start of 12th Street is Café Texan. Apparently a hit with the locals, I'd come across it whilst researching and I eat there the first day. It's basically a greasy spoon and they still allow you to smoke inside. The waitress constantly has a fag on the whole time I'm there.

Then you have Walker County Court, a theatre, the Greyhound bus station, and finally right at the top of 12th Street, you'll find the Huntsville Unit itself, or 'Walls Unit' as its nicknamed, due to the really massive walls.

Here you'll mainly find general-population prisoners serving out their time, but also behind those high walls in the east corner you will find the death house.

Beat.

Sandy has to work, take care of her son and spend time with a family who are about to lose their dad to the lethal injection, so my first twenty-four hours in Huntsville are spent by myself, which I actually don't mind. I have a car and a sat nav.

It's an uneventful twenty-four hours. Apart from having to change motel.

Stabbing action and Psycho *shower noise.*

Obviously Sandy and I have different levels of safety and cleanliness.

Everything is familiar yet also not quite right and therefore hard work.

Asking for a bin, 'Have you got a bin? A bin, a bin,' and getting no response until you say trash can.

Not being served alcohol in a restaurant as you've left your ID in the motel and the girl asking you is young enough to be your daughter.

Driving on the wrong but well the right side of the road. Cars turning right even when the traffic light is on red.

A margarita in a pint glass.

And biscuits and gravy for breakfast. I wouldn't want that at any time of day.

We may all be speaking English, but we are speaking a very different language.

I text Stompy some of these brilliant, witty insights. I think he'll find them funny.

Text message on screen.

'Please come home.'

Picture of cat.

7 – Juan's Execution

So, I'm sat in Mr Hamburger –

See picture of STEPH *in Mr Hamburger.*

in Huntsville. It's just after 4 p.m. I'm meeting Sandy in an hour at the Walls Unit. If all goes to plan tonight thirty-five-year-old Juan Rodriguez is set to be executed.

Aside from the freaky Mr Hamburger sign –

Image of the sign.

it looks an okay place to eat, close to where I'm meeting Sandy, I can actually see the unit from here.

It isn't lost on me that right now that Juan Rodriguez will be eating his last meal. It's a myth that they can choose anything they want. They can't, not in Texas anyway, they can only choose from what the prison is serving that day. And even if they have an appetite their stomach contents will shortly fill an autopsy dish.

Video of protestors outside prison.

At 5:15 I make my way over to the intersection outside the Walls Unit. I thought being here would help the research but I feel like an execution tourist. There are about fifteen people gathered. Some are family of Juan Rodriguez. Some are anti-death-penalty protestors. That woman in blue is Sandy. I –

Gestures a wave.

and she nods her acknowledgement.

I watch Juan Rodriguez's children hide their red, blotchy faces behind bright-pink placards, which proudly display their father's picture and the words 'execution is not the solution'. I find out that Sandy provides these at each execution. She replaces the picture with the inmate being executed that day and so they get rolled out each time.

I watch the general-population inmates watch us through the barred windows and wonder what they make of us. The prison will go on lockdown just before the execution starts.

It's now six o'clock and beyond the caution tape down the block, we see Juan Rodriguez's witnesses cross the road and enter the main building. Sandy thrusts a flameless candle in my hand covered in religious sentiment.

She reads out a poem written for this occasion by another inmate. It's basic and naive but in this moment I have to fight to contain the emotion it stirs. And then a priest rings a bell fifteen times, once for each year Juan Rodriguez was on death row. His daughter's sobs become unbearable and she cries out 'My dad has gone. I can't believe my dad has gone.'

Just over a hundred metres away from where we stand, state-sanctioned homicide has taken place in revenge for a murder and the theft of eight dollars.

8 – First Visit Jonny

Video of road to Livingston.

The next day I take the road out to Livingston. This is the road that will take me to the Polunsky Unit, where death row is housed. This is the road that will take me to Jonny.

And I won't get to feel his breath on my face, or know how it feels to hold him or touch his skin or know his smell but I'll be able to hear his voice and see his smile and look into his eyes. And yes, it will be through bulletproof glass and down a phone, but it will be the closest I've ever been to him.

Video montage of the road.

Once out of Huntsville and overlooking the fact there is some sort of church every hundred metres and they all have religious warnings such as 'You think it's hot now, just wait' and 'Walmart is not the only saving place', and the run-down trailer parks, and strange shops and eateries and the pawn shops which offer cash for guns and of course the gun shops and the concealed-gun classes and being looked at like you're foreign and the roadkill which is plentiful and large and the dog that runs out on me and I only miss by an inch and good luck despite all of this despite all of this, it's a beautiful drive.

Especially when you get to Lake Livingston.

Image of Lake Livingston.

Jonny will be driven to his execution across this lake on the last day of his life. He will see the beauty of the world and a snapshot of life happening along this forty-five-mile stretch of road. Life which has moved on without him in those fourteen years he has been locked up. Life which is no longer concerned with him or is his concern.

At first I drive straight past the entrance to the Polunsky Unit. I don't know what I wanted but is this it? Look at it.

See the prison from a distance.

An unimaginative building with tiny windows which are probably filthy and you can't see through. And I bet they don't clean them. Oh Christ has this been Jonny's view for the last fourteen years? How is he not a dribbling, deranged psychopath? Well he probably is, he probably is I've probably come all this way to come face to face with a murdering nutter. Why am I not at home drinking too much coffee making stories up with the cat? Why couldn't I have settled for that? Because I'm never satisfied that's why, because I always want more, because Jonny asked me to come, because I wanted to come, because I want to meet Jonny, because I feel I have to meet Jonny.

And I am being ridiculous, I am, because none of Jonny's letters have had dried dribble on and they are all very coherent, intelligent, witty, beautiful at times. I need to be able to rationalise this intelligent funny man I correspond with, with the man who shot and killed a convenience-store worker in the heat of a robbery. A crime so terrible that the state of Texas feel the only fitting punishment is for him to pay with his life.

I spend some time being interfered with by the guards and doing everything I'm asked before eventually arriving at the visitation hall, with a clear bag containing twenty dollars in coins so I can buy Jonny food and drink from the vending machines. I sit and stare through bulletproof glass at a little empty cubicle waiting for Jonny to be brought through. I watch men in dressed in regulation white with their arms handcuffed behind them being brought up to meet loved ones, eager to start their two-hour visit, not wanting to miss a second of it. And then the door behind the bulletproof glass opens.

Jonny.

There is this really awkward wait whilst he offers his hands to the gap in the door and the guard takes his cuffs off. I don't know where to look but I can't look away. Jonny smiles as we both pick up the phones we'll talk through. I don't know what to say. I don't know what to say. I don't know what to say.

'You came,' he says and smiles and my stomach flips.

9 – Time in Texas

Voice-over of women and men's images.

'He's one of the most attractive people I have ever seen in my life.'

'He looks like a mythical Western figure you might read about.'

'No woman has ever gotten a love letter until they have gotten a love letter from a man in prison.'

'His letters are like dates.'

'He's a fallen angel.'

'It was a beautiful courtship.'

'If I saw him walking down the street I'd feel the same.'

'He's a blessing.'

STEPH *rips pictures of Juan Rodriguez off bright-pink placards as seen in the film with the protestors. She balls them up and throws them at the bin. Generally, she misses the bin.*

Over the month I am in Texas I get to see Jonny every week. Sometimes it's just us, sometimes his sister is there too, which is nice.

Beat.

Communication with Stompy is restricted to –

Text messages on screen.

'Have you been raped mugged and murdered and thrown in a ditch yet?'

Picture of cat.

'Tiggy is stress-licking. Had to put his jumper on.'

'Next door's children keep asking where you are and when you'll be home. What should I tell them?'

Sandy keeps me busy, really busy. She's always going on about how there wasn't enough time for Jonny and I to marry.

She takes me to all these anti-death-penalty protests and rallies where hardly anybody turns up. I find Sandy putting words into my mouth.

STEPH *on film as if being interviewed.*

'Some people will be beyond rehabilitation.

Some people may argue against rehabilitation and prefer a life for a life. But as many protestors quote, 'should society kill those who kill to show killing is wrong?'

After one interview Sandy gives me some media training Sandy-style. She says I'm on-message but not bringing it back to Jonny enough. I have to mention him more. He needs to be at the forefront of any argument I make. This is all about Jonny.

For a bit of, errr, respite? I take a ride out here.

STEPH *outside Texas Prison Museum.*

The Texas Prison Museum. I get to see exhibits such as this one.

Inmate shanks image.

Shanks made by prisoners and I learn about the prison rodeo –

Rodeo image.

they used to do at the Walls Unit and I see the actual gun –

Gun image.

found on Bonnie and Clyde's bodies. Rounding a corner I come face to face with this.

Texas electric chair image.

'Old Sparky.' The actual Texas electric chair. People who visit the museum ask to sit in it. They want to sit where three hundred and sixty-one men met their end.

Exiting through the gift shop I buy the following –

Items are pulled out of a box.

An Old Sparky shot glass.

An 'I Did Time in Huntsville' hat.

Puts hat on.

Mini-handcuffs key ring.

Some other bits I won't bore you with.

And these which are actually for a small dog but will totally fit the cat.

Holds up a mini-Stetson and boots.

There are numerous items made by inmates of the TDCJ, purses, wallets, belt buckles, dominoes. This list goes on. I don't select any of these.

10 – Execution Day

On the morning of the execution.

Realises she still has the 'I Did Time in Huntsville' hat on. Takes it off and starts again.

On the morning of the execution we get a final visit with Jonny. He is calmer than me, much calmer. He says it's not goodbye, that he's sure will meet again in the next life. I don't believe that but I'm not about to argue it out with a man with only hours left to live. As time is called he places his hand on the glass and I place mine to meet his. It's a heroic goodbye filled with hope, despair and the grief that the next few hours will bring.

Jonny will be driven to Huntsville around lunchtime. The exact time is kept under wraps in case anyone tries to break him out.

Sandy is counting down the hours with the family so I take myself here.

Image of Lake Livingston.

The lake is beautiful and still. There's a large group of small turtles scavenging near the surface of the water. The sun is warm and high. Cars pass backwards and forwards across the bridge. No sign of the van or Jonny or the crocodiles that reportedly like to hang out in this lake.

Would a crocodile eat the turtles? Yes, I suppose.

This isn't the first time I've felt this crippling sense of helplessness. I'm transported four thousand miles back home. My brother has gone missing. What do you mean, missing? How can an adult be missing? But he's a vulnerable adult and no one knows where he is. He's walked out of the home he shares with my parents. He says he's not coming back. He says he's gonna end it all, this is it this time. And all you can do is keep ringing him until he answers one of your calls so you can start pleading with him 'please come home, please come home.'

Sat on the edge of Lake Livingston there is no one to call, no one to plead with. It's all been done. It's just me and the turtles waiting for Jonny and the van.

Pause.

We sit in a building just over the road from the Walls Unit waiting to be taken across. Someone chunners constantly. I don't know if it is at me, I don't know what they say. I don't hear them. There still could be a stay of execution. There's still time. There still must be time.

At six o'clock the warden will get the official go-ahead. He will make his way to the holding cell with the tie-down team and he will tell Jonny it's time to follow him into the next room. Jonny said he will go willingly. No struggle. No fight.

He will be asked to get up on the gurney and then lie down with his head on the pillow. Within seconds of him being horizontal the tie-down team will strap him in place. His arms outstretched. The IVs will be placed into them and wrapped in bandages. A white sheet will cover his body, leaving his neck and head exposed. The victim's witnesses will be led into their witness room along with a smattering of press. The door will be locked behind them.

And only when this is done do they come for us. We are led across the road. In the distance I can hear the protestors where I stood, what, only a month ago. We enter the Walls Unit, turn left and walk down an outside corridor bathed in sunshine. We are led into our viewing room and the door gets locked behind us. The curtain is drawn back to reveal Jonny on the gurney. There's no two-way glass here and he can see both us and the victim's witnesses next door. We only hear their murmurs and shuffles. He looks at me and he tentatively smiles. The warden reads the death warrant and asks Jonny if he wishes to make a final statement.

I'm in Blackpool on the seafront. It's a grey windy night.

'You have to live and die by the choices you make.'

I don't feel the cold, I'm heated by alcohol.

'I'm sorry for the pain I have caused.'

I hang over the sea wall and let the spray hit me.

'I send love to my sister, family and friends.'

The sea is black. But its murky water looks welcoming.

'Know I go to a better place.'

I wonder what it would be like to lie on its surface, push off from the side and drift.

'I love you all.'

Letting the waves carry me on and on and on.

'Warden, I'm ready.'

Pause.

Time of death as 6:29 p.m. Sandy lets out a massive sob and we're led out into blinding sunshine.

11 – Aftermath

I've witnessed this scene before through a screen, four thousand miles away from here. Sat on my sofa with my cat and Stompy.

The body dressed in regulation white filling a cheap coffin in the funeral home. The woman crying over her man as if he were a soldier fallen in some pointless war, a hero in death.

The first time I kiss his lips they're soft and still warm. He has a bead of sweat on his forehead. Perhaps it is a tear left by Sandy. He feels clammy. I trace the lines of his tattoos on his arm with my finger. Tattoos I had sat and looked at through a bullet-proof window hour after hour wondering what his arms would feel like under my touch. And now I know. I take his hand in mine. The hand that held a gun, the fingers which pulled the trigger. The hand, the body of a killer, now dead at the hands of the state.

I'm not sure what I am supposed to feel in this moment, but I'm surprised to feel nothing.

Back at the motel Sandy has gone out drinking with the family. I have a bottle and am okay with my own company. I want to phone home. I want to hear Stompy's voice, but it's late back home, maybe it's too late. I send him a text.

Text messages on screen.

'You awake? xxx'

'No.'

'How you texting then? xxx'

'They killed him?'

'Yes xxx'

It says 'read'. He doesn't respond.

I want to listen to my mum ramble on about my brother and what he has or hasn't done or some new system at her work I don't fully understand. I want to sit in silence with my dad and watch a film he's seen millions of time, *Where Eagles Dare*, or *Bridge Over the River Kwai*. I want to talk about Marvel with my brother. I want to be sat on the sofa dying for the toilet, but I can't possibly move as the cat is asleep on my knee. And I want to be in mine and Stompy's home; whatever is left of mine and Stompy's home.

12 – What Happens Now?

On the way to the airport I stop here.

Images of statue of Sam Houston.

The Sam Houston statue and visitor centre. He was a big deal in Texas. They boast this is the tallest statue of an American hero. Is that even a thing? Who knew? But they would brag about that, wouldn't they, as it's America and everything is big and brilliant. I didn't google him, I'm sure you can if you're interested.

And it's ridiculous, completely ridiculous but overlooking a highway with a giant statue behind me feels like the perfect place to read Jonny's final letter.

'If you are reading this my love then the Texas killing machine has had its revenge. Don't be sad about my passing. Know I am in a better, happier place.

Our love has had the most positive effect on me and brought much joy in these final months. It has been unlike the other romantic relationships I have had with a pen pal. My only regret is I couldn't get divorced in time to marry you.

I know I said I would sign over half of the money in my trust fund to help your costs but Sandy is in great need so I hope you will forgive me, my love, for signing it all over to her.

I hate the thought of you going back to Stompy or being with anyone else but I understand what is like to go without comfort and the touch of another and you must do what's best for you.

Know that your sweet face was the last image I held onto as I drifted away.

I'll be on our ranch in the sky waiting for you to join me when you're ready.'

Pause.

He told me in his first letter he had never had a romantic relationship with a pen pal.

A divorce? No one mentioned he needed a divorce.

Pause.

I send Stompy a text –

On screen:

'I'm on my way to the airport. I'm coming home xx'

We see the three dots appear and disappear as Stompy goes to reply and then doesn't.

He's replying.

He's not replying.

If I was him I'd probably be like, 'What do you want, a marching band and banner?'

Stompy isn't like that though.

Text message on screen:

'I know I've fucked up, I'm sorry.'

Text message on screen:

'I need to come home and we need to talk. If you want I'll move back to my mum and dad's for a bit. But I'm coming home first. It is still my home.'

Well if we are over I will probably have to go back up north and get a one-bedroom flat that would take me and the cat.

And I'd need to get a part-time job. Temping or something.

Maybe I should write a comedy next. My mum's always saying, 'Why don't you just write a comedy?' Something which doesn't involve death or too much research. Maybe.

The cat and I would have to make new friends but actually it doesn't feel like it would be the end of the world. I mean I know it's not ideal, but we'd be alright, we would, we'd be alright.

The following exchange takes place through text messages on the screen:

'You're a dick'

'That's not new information. xx'

'I'm sorry. xx'

'Yeah, you said. It doesn't change anything.'

'No. xx'

'You fell in love with a murderer and went halfway round the world to marry him.'

'I wasn't in love with him and I didn't get married. xx'

'So you've finally realised none of it was real.'

'It wasn't as straightforward as that. It's hard to explain. I can't do it over text. xx'

'The cat hasn't been right the whole time you've been gone.'

'Have you given him lots of cuddles and treats? xx'

'Of course.'

'I've missed you both xx'

No answer.

'Will you be home when I get back? xx'

'I may be flying to California to meet a woman in prison.'

'Please don't be like that xx'

'I haven't been sat here just waiting for you, you know.'

'What do you mean? xx'

'I've been getting out meeting new people.'

'So you've met someone? xx'

'I didn't say that.'

'Look, I'm tired. I can't do this. Let's sort things when I get back. xx'

'What is there to sort?'

'Us, I would hope. xx'

No reply.

'Will you meet me at the airport? xx'

'You are fucking outrageous'

'But you'll come? xx'

Long pause.

'Yes'

The End.

WHITE LEAD

Jessica Siân

'I have already settled it for myself so
flattery and criticism go down the same drain'

Georgia O'Keeffe

Characters

DIDO
VENNI
CAROL

VENNI *and* CAROL *stand, facing off across a dining table.*
DIDO *is sat at the table between them.*

Beat.

DIDO. Wine anyone?

VENNI. Yes.   CAROL. No.

CAROL. She shouldn't –

VENNI. She's fine. You're fine aren't you Dido?

DIDO. I'll go and get it.

VENNI. Not far then?

CAROL. No not –

VENNI. B&B? Or what is it now? AirBnB –

CAROL. No actually, Karl –

VENNI. Karl?

CAROL. Don't get –

VENNI. Karl? Well –

CAROL. It's nothing…

VENNI. No, no, just, well I only see him, what? Every other
    day, in here every other day, poking about the studio, rubbing
    his nose in a canvas, fingering through some –

CAROL. It's not ideal I –

VENNI. Report back does he?

CAROL. No, he –

VENNI. Space. That's what you said wasn't it? Space? Yes?

CAROL. Yes?

VENNI. Hm, sounds like you've got what you wanted then.

CAROL. We keep it separate, he... I've asked him not to mention –

VENNI. Karl not talk about... Ha, what else does Karl Rippen have to talk about?

CAROL. Nothing, it's not –

VENNI. No, really, I'm curious, what do you discuss? What's dinner conversation round Karl's?

CAROL. I don't know, general... stuff, things that happen, telly –

VENNI. Telly!? One of the UK's foremost art dealers is in to *Strictly* this season is he?

CAROL. Do you have to be so –

VENNI. Who's he supporting then? Do you watch it together? Share a packet of digestives?

CAROL. Jesus! Can you just... He's just letting me stay, I asked him not to tell you, I knew you'd make him feel horrible about it and you know he'll do anything for you –

VENNI. He'll do anything for the work something you –

CAROL. Yeah okay, fine. I walked out on you, I walked out on 'the work'. I'm at Karl's okay? Can we drop it?

Beat.

VENNI. Well you can tell him I found some preparatory sketches from '89 –

CAROL. No –

VENNI. The year Dido came, I did this whole series of –

CAROL. I'm not here to talk about the retrospective Venni I'm here for Dido.

VENNI. Fine, fine... Do you know why she's...?

CAROL. No. Something she's got to, I don't know, tell us... together.

VENNI. She's cooking.

CAROL. Dinner?

VENNI. I'm not sure if it's good or bad. She looks good. Seems healthy.

CAROL. Last time she cooked she was fourteen and she'd shot up one of your canvases with her air rifle... Lasagne I think.

DIDO. 'Figure Three, Greek Street', part of series wasn't it? Really... you used some special –

VENNI. Yes, well, long time ago.

DIDO. I've not brought my air rifle, so... not to worry. Red alright?

VENNI. Are you going to put us out of our misery then?

DIDO. In a bit, can we just –

CAROL. Give her a minute.

DIDO. Thanks, just, yeah... what are you working on?

VENNI. Red's lovely, Carol?

CAROL. I'm fine.

VENNI. I'm not allowed to talk about work.

CAROL. Don't be a child.

> VENNI *pours two large glasses of red wine and shoves one into* CAROL*'s hand.* CAROL *puts it down... picks it up, has a sip, puts it back down.*

> It's a retrospective, a gallery in Berlin's... well it's an honour to be asked and your mother, as always, has somehow managed to find a way to be infuriated by the whole thing.

VENNI. It's not a 'retrospective' it's a fucking autopsy. Picking through my own bones is what it is.

CAROL. See.

VENNI. That's the, that's why she walked out she –

CAROL. No, it's not, I was very clear about –

VENNI. Can't understand, has never been able to really grasp what it costs me.

CAROL. And what about what it costs me, Venni?

VENNI. I'm sure prepping canvases is exhausting.

CAROL. Oh just, Dido I'm... I'm sorry I'll just... I'll just... out for a cigarette, is that? I mean is dinner?

DIDO. No there's, that's, there's time.

CAROL. Fine... Don't fucking tell her anything, okay? Not while I'm gone, okay?

DIDO. Okay.

CAROL. Okay.

CAROL *goes to leave, she trips on the edge of a canvas.*

Jesus fuck!

Exits.

DIDO. Couldn't find a mug.

VENNI. Hm?

DIDO. Paint, turps in the bottom of all of them.

VENNI. Right, I uh... I need to get somebody round, cleaner or...

DIDO. New mugs?

VENNI. Right. She just can't, god I know I'm not always easy but... I'm in the middle of it, I just I need to be... just, I'm in the middle of it.

DIDO. Yeah I know.

VENNI. You do?

DIDO. When I was making that one-woman show, remember? I was like, just, totally unavailable.

VENNI. Is that why you... have you made another...?

DIDO. Oh, no, that wasn't, I mean I was still looking for my medium so...

VENNI. Right.

DIDO. So this retrospective?

VENNI. It's a chance to show some new work no one's interested in, well except Karl, bless him, he made it part of the deal.

DIDO. What's wrong with it?

VENNI. It's not the old work. God forbid you should ever be liked darling... I didn't mean, I mean be successful.

DIDO. Right.

VENNI. What's for dinner?

DIDO. Lasagne.

...

CAROL *and* VENNI *are sat across from each other at the table,* DIDO *is stood, a manuscript on the table before her. No sign of dinner.*

CAROL. It's just...

DIDO. Thanks.

CAROL. I'm so... I mean really it's...

DIDO. Thanks.

VENNI. *Flattery and Criticism*?

DIDO. Yeah.

VENNI. Is that?

DIDO. It's something Georgia O'Keeffe –

VENNI. 'I've settled it for myself so flattery and criticism go down the same drain.'

DIDO. Exactly. You used to... when I was younger it was something you used to –

VENNI. Say, yes.

CAROL. Well I think it's great. Can I...?

DIDO. Yeah, uh I, I mean I'll get you both copies, when it's you know… and signed and –

CAROL. That's, it's just wonderful Di, we're so proud of you.

DIDO. Thanks I'm really, you know I think I've finally found my, you know, like, thing.

CAROL. Passion?

DIDO. Exactly.

VENNI. What's it about?

DIDO. Well actually it's inspired by, I mean you know, write what you know and –

VENNI. Gotta get published.

DIDO. What?

CAROL. Venni.

VENNI. I'm just saying, one of those stickers they put… what are they called, they must have a name? Those stickers you see on books? You know the ones, on books in Tescos? 'Richard & Judy Bookclub' or –

DIDO. No –

VENNI. Yours could be: 'Based on the life of the daughter of Venni Lanois' –

DIDO. It's not… I'm not doing that.

CAROL. Jesus Christ Ven it's not about you.

VENNI. It's not?

CAROL. I mean the issue, the… Dido's written a book, a getting-published book for Christ's, this moment isn't about you.

VENNI. Might be about you?

CAROL. What?

VENNI. Is it about her? You were around more, in the, how old were you when Carol became part of our little family? Six?

CAROL. Well if I've been an influence then I'm flattered.

DIDO. Just... I want, it's very important to me that you both read it, that you... you know feedback I guess or –

VENNI. And if we don't like it?

CAROL. We'll like it. I'll like it.

VENNI. You'll say you do. Like with the acting and the photography and the, what was it? Silkscreening before that.

DIDO. I was trying to find my –

CAROL. I don't like all of your work.

VENNI. Yes, you've recently become brutally honest about that. You were a little less truthful in the past... when we met for instance... gushy –

CAROL. Oh for –

VENNI. Swooning even.

CAROL. I was young, I was intimidated, Christ I was your fucking student.

VENNI. Blinded by love, blinded to my... what did you call it? 'Puerile use of white lead.'

CAROL. Don't put words in my mouth.

VENNI. What are you doing here?

CAROL. .... Dido –

VENNI. You wanted to see how I was managing without you. Hm? Well I'm not, I'm not managing.

CAROL. Then you should hire someone. Send me a copy love I'll –

VENNI. Using a pseudonym?

DIDO. No, not –

VENNI. Dido Lanois Lieberwitz?

DIDO. So? I mean, what do you care if it is about you? You don't give a fuck what people think, that's what you say, what people think about Venni the woman. Only Venni the work, a 'Lanois', that's what you care about.

CAROL. It's about me?

DIDO. No Carol it's not –

CAROL. Lieberwitz? When did you start using… I'm in it?

DIDO. I just thought you'd…

CAROL. What?

DIDO. Like it.

CAROL. Right.

CAROL *fills her wine glass, drinks long and slowly.*

VENNI. I'm fucking starving.

CAROL. What about me?

VENNI. What are we looking at here Di? Twenty minutes? Half an hour?

DIDO. Not… there's no specific, I mean people, I guess people could read into certain –

VENNI. Get an olive at least or –

CAROL. I came to get you.

DIDO. I know.

CAROL. Twice.

DIDO. I know. Carol I'm not –

CAROL. I'm what? I'm fodder now?

DIDO. No –

CAROL. For your creative, what? Endeavour? Jesus.

DIDO. It's just a book, you're practically Venni's slave –

CAROL. Watch your mouth.

DIDO. I made something didn't I? That's what you want from me. That's what I'm supposed to do?

VENNI. Off your own back, you gonna create something you
    make it off your own back not off my reputation, our
    relationship.

DIDO. What about you? You don't use her?

VENNI. Carol is my assistant and my partner –

DIDO. Oh please –

VENNI. You have gone behind our backs –

DIDO. It's not a conspiracy –

VENNI. Not a thought for how we might feel or –

DIDO. Feel?! –

VENNI. Didn't think to consult –

DIDO. Madonna and child –

VENNI. That's different –

DIDO. Eighty-eight to ninety-two –

VENNI. That series was about me not –

DIDO. You adopted me! To paint me. I'm your walking talking
    fucking art project Venni!

CAROL. Something's burning.

VENNI. Fuck's sake Dido.

    Exit VENNI.

                    …

CAROL *and* DIDO *sit with a burnt lasagne before them.*

CAROL. Might be alright underneath?

DIDO. Might give us cancer.

CAROL. Well in that case…

    CAROL *rolls a cigarette.*

DIDO. When did you leave?

CAROL. Six weeks ago I guess.

DIDO. Didn't call.

CAROL. No.

DIDO. Because you thought you'd come back?

CAROL. I don't know Dido... because I didn't want to think about it.

DIDO. Are you fucking Karl?

CAROL. Would that be good for your book?

DIDO. You gave up your whole life for Venni –

CAROL. That's not –

DIDO. Your own art –

CAROL. I was never very good.

DIDO. Having kids?

CAROL. I am a mother –

DIDO. I know.

CAROL. I'm your mother.

DIDO. I know. But what, all of a sudden it's just too hard?

CAROL. Do you know what white lead is Dido?

DIDO. Paint.

CAROL. Pigment, beautiful, luminous, you'll see it in classical European oil paintings, seventeenth century, it radiates from the canvas. Almost impossible to get now, it's toxic, breathing it in. The artists knew, they knew it was killing them, seeping into their clothes, sticking to their hair, polluting their homes, making their children ill, their loved ones, their whores, but they still used it. It was so beautiful they didn't care.

VENNI. I wear a mask.

CAROL. It's a fucking metaphor.

VENNI. Please don't smoke that in here.

CAROL. Dido's practically burnt the house down and you've got the whole place smelling like turps... Fine.

CAROL *puts her fag down and pours herself more wine.*

VENNI. I've ordered pizza.

DIDO. I might just go actually.

CAROL. Drop the bomb and off you go.

DIDO. You obviously aren't going to –

CAROL. No responsibility –

DIDO. She doesn't take responsibility –

CAROL. That's true –

DIDO. With the work you make the people you suck the... what are they, drain the –

CAROL. Succubus –

DIDO. Thank you, leave empty –

VENNI. The people in my portraits aren't hurt by my painting them –

DIDO. Not them, not them, us. Me, Carol, fucking Karl, and now the shoe's on the other foot –

CAROL. Settle it for yourself –

DIDO. Exactly, but that only applies to you, to your work –

VENNI. You can't just take something I said and –

DIDO. Writing this book has made me well... got me... given me clarity. I shouldn't've asked, should have just put it out, got it out there, been like you and not cared what –

VENNI. This isn't care this is you seeking approval –

DIDO. And why would I want that? How absurd for me to want you... to want my... you to see me.

CAROL. Mother.

DIDO. What?

CAROL. Your mother to see you.

DIDO. Right.

CAROL. You won't remember but when you were little you did used to call her Mum, you used to and she would tell you off. She'd say: 'What's your name?' and you'd say: 'Dido.' 'And what's my name?' 'Venni.' 'And who's that?' 'Carol.' 'Good, yes, Venni and Carol, good girl.' God and so admired that, I so badly wanted to be a part of that, that… casting-off. And yet here we are, you looking for approval, me begging for scraps and Ven… desperate to get back to the studio. Aren't you?

VENNI. I have to do it. I have to do it I have to do it I have to do it. I am not trying to hurt you but I have to do it. I love you, your fucking skin, your, but I have to do it.

DIDO. Right, like exactly, me to, that why this whole book thing is –

CAROL. What if I came back?

VENNI. Great, that's what I want, that would be –

CAROL. Not to the commission. Just to you. Not to work. What if I came back just to you?

VENNI. Well I…

CAROL. And you have to give me time.

VENNI. What sort of –

CAROL. Two weeks, two weeks a year when you don't even think about work –

VENNI. I don't know how to promise not to think –

CAROL. Just two weeks!

VENNI. I can't give you –

CAROL. I'm getting out of here, you're, you're both succubus… succubi… fuck…

CAROL *goes to leave,* DIDO *grabs the wine bottle.*

DIDO. Carol!

VENNI. Put that down.

CAROL. Are you threatening me?

DIDO. Don't go.

CAROL. Or?

VENNI. Come on babe, don't go, just... sit down.

CAROL. Or what? Or what Dido?

DIDO. I just want you to read it.

CAROL. If you mean it, if you've made this and you mean it then you don't need anything from me. I can't do this any more.

DIDO. I'll do it.

CAROL. Go on then.

> DIDO *presses the bottle to her lips, she can't face it, she pours the remainder of the bottle over her head.*

...

VENNI. Sit down babe, come on, don't leave like this, come and sit down.

> CAROL *waits in the doorway.*

> Pizza's on its way, let's just... let's at least fucking... (*Opening the manuscript.*) 'The house had been restored once, some time before, but looking at it now you couldn't tell...'

> *Lights.*

WHAT IS THE CUSTOM OF YOUR GRIEF?

Timberlake Wertenbaker

Characters

ZARGHONA
EMILY

ZARGHONA. My dear friend, hi Emily,

> Forgive me if this is not the courteous way to address you.
> I am not assured what is correct form of address because
> I am learning English. I am thanking you for accepting my
> friendship request on Facebook. You are my only English.
> I see you are online, I am in internet café in Quetta but I
> have only half-hour so maybe I go silent rapidly.

EMILY. Hey Zarghona,

> Yeah I'm chatting because I'm not at school – because
> I don't want to think right now. Or feel

> I thought you were a girl I used to know – Isn't Quetta in
> Pakistan?

ZARGHONA. Hey Emily,

> I write on your private wall now please and you too to mine.
> Yes Quetta is in Pakistan we have come from Afghanistan
> some years ago.

EMILY. Weird. Do you know Helmand? How did you find me?

ZARGHONA. I think you are asking with what permission do
I call myself your friend? It is because of your sadness. I saw
on internet your brother died yesterday. They say there is a
sister at school and I think perhaps you are my age and I
search your name on Facebook. I understand your sadness
Emily because I believe I too lost my brother yesterday at
the time of yours.

EMILY. Don't you know? I know – I just can't believe it. Is that
what you mean?

ZARGHONA. News not clear. But I know.

EMILY. Yeah. We didn't hear from him for a while. I knew.

ZARGHONA. Maybe we share a lot.

EMILY. Not sure I can share this with anyone. Maybe.

ZARGHONA. I think we help each other. I have questions.
How did you hear about your brother? I want to imagine
your hours. And tell me, Emily when you lose a loved one in
your country, what is the custom of your grief? Maybe if
I know I have help because I am a sister like you. My nem
saat is up. That means half-hour in Pashto.

TIME

EMILY. No one thinks about sisters. Everyone is worrying
about my mother. Tim's fiancée is being asked questions on
TV. Nobody asks me what I feel. Tim was my only brother,
I shared all my life with him. That life, me, it's like, wiped
out. I can't talk to anyone, my mother's gone far away
somewhere. My friends feel sorry and then they don't know
what to say and ask if I want to go out and have a good time.
Don't they get it?

ZARGHONA. Hey Emily

I see only the women of my family and they don't get it
because I am young and my culture does not believe my
feelings are advanced. Only you can know what they are.
I sit in internet café now. I think about that moment I hear
about my brother and life turns a catapult.

EMILY. I know what you mean. This officer we'd never seen
before came to the door, full uniform and he wasn't smiling.
We were having tea and when my mum saw him she tried to
stop him saying anything. She started talking about all the
roses she was planting – there's a famous rose-grower here
in Norfolk where we live. She described the roses, the
names, the colours, whether they were climbers or ramblers
or scramblers or shrubs and he waited patiently until she ran
out of roses and told us. I held my stomach. And then she
offered him tea. It's a custom in our country when we don't
know what to do or say we ask people if they want some tea.
And then we ask about milk. And sugar. And biscuits and the
whole time there's this dark hole underneath and everyone
pretends it's not there and he accepted the tea. We call it a
stiff upper lip. Have you got those in your culture? How did
you hear about your brother? What happened?

ZARGHONA. I like this expression stiff upper lip. Why do you hide your grief? Is it because of danger? But it is good to have a real person. My father only had phone call. He went even more quiet than quiet and then he turned to my mother and said our son is in the hands of god and then he said he was a little injured, a motorbike accident and they would bring him to Cheman for treatment and god is good and she must stay calm and then I knew. And this hurt in stomach. I have only one brother, like you, I live because of him, he taught me English and we have all our secrets together. And so I know my father will have another phone call and tell my mother the motorcycle accident is more serious. Cheman is only a few hours away. There will be a car but maybe I am wrong.

EMILY. We are also waiting for the car. Tim's been flown from Helmand to a place called RAF Lyneham this morning and the drive takes about five hours. Mum is making all the preparations for the funeral. It keeps her busy, she can't even cry, she's on the phone all the time, I sit alone in my room. I think about Tim.

ZARGHONA. I can only sit alone in internet café because at home we have one room for sleep and being, but I am worried because the shopkeeper maybe notices. I tell my parents I am shopping for food and I do that too. Today I will make potatoes with onions and tomatoes and our spices which are cumin and mint. Emily, your brother like my brother is martyr, does he go to Paradise in your culture?

EMILY. Our martyrs are people in paintings with a lot of arrows through them, it was a long time ago when no one was allowed to believe in the Christian god or something. I was crap at RE. Why is your brother a martyr if he died in a motorcycle accident?

ZARGHONA. RE is what?

EMILY. You study religion.

ZARGHONA. Like we study Koran.

EMILY. Not quite, you sort of shop around religions looking at stuff here and there. I ended up not knowing anything.

What the newspapers and everyone calls my brother is a hero. I guess it's sort of religious too. Not sure about Paradise. So why is your brother a martyr?

ZARGHONA. I am in new café with nice shopkeeper. In our culture, we call martyr anyone who does not die a natural death. I tell you about motorcycle accident another time. I think so much about Ajmal. He was very good student, he loved our pistachio nuts, he likes music and we watch American films secretly.

EMILY. Tim loved languages, he was studying French and Russian. I didn't get what made him join the army. We aren't a military family. It was almost like he wanted the army like a gap year and he stayed.

ZARGHONA. There are so many words I do not understand, forgive this stupidness, what is gap year? By military family do you mean like our tribe. We too are not military tribe but all Pashtuns have honour. But Ajmal I think he was head-hot.

EMILY. A gap year you spend travelling because you're fed up with school and it helps you grow up. So they say.

ZARGHONA. How can you be too full of going to school? Girls here not much allowed and I only want education and better English. I love English poetry, I get your poet laurel Carol Ann Duffy on internet.

EMILY. If you'd been through the English school system you'd be fed up. Tim was very stubborn. He loved adventure and he was very sporty.

ZARGHONA. Sporty?

EMILY. Loves sweating.

ZARGHONA. Like in football? Ajmal loved football and did very good volleyball.

EMILY. Tim liked windsurfing, canoeing, mountain-climbing but he also played the guitar.

ZARGHONA. Ajmal played the Rabab. I think it is like your guitar.

We do not respect musicians in our culture but it is all right to play the Rabab.

EMILY. You don't respect musicians? We worship them!!!

I hear the car. It's Tim. Got to Go.

TIME

ZARGHONA. My dear friend Emily.

Yesterday the car came to us and they brought my brother's body to our house. He had died in Cheman. We have to bury him quickly according to Muslim custom, but only then could we have the grave dug because we have to be careful not to attract attention. We do not offer tea to anyone but I would like to share how we make grief. And then you will tell me about you and I will feel less alone.

They lay Ajmal on the bed to wait till nightfall. We do not wash his body because he is martyr and he is in his clothes of death because the blood is holy.

But now at last we the women of the family can cry and we uncover our heads even with the men there and we pull our hair and we beat our chests. All this pain I try to beat and pull out of me but it is only good for a moment. Then we say good things about him that he is kind and generous and he respects his elders and his parents but I cannot say about Rabab and football and films. When grave is ready we cover him with green cloth with Koran verses embroidered. Now the men will carry the body to the graveyard but we women only accompany the body to the door. And Emily my heart is pulled out of me as I go to edge of threshold, I want to hold him back and cling him to me but I am not allowed. I watch as they walk quickly to graveyard, quiet not to attract gossip. And then we women cry more and tell more good things about him and then someone says be calm, it is the will of god, and he is martyr and goes to Paradise but how can I be calm when he will never be with me again. We were very loving brother and sister. Who understands this love? Only you, Emily, but in the last year he became more quiet and angry. I know your car was yesterday too, I think of you.

EMILY. Hey Zarghona, I'm glad I can talk to you.

I wish I could have seen my brother's body I think it would have helped me believe he was dead. But all that is done in Helmand, I don't even know what he was wearing. All we got was the coffin wrapped in the British flag, at least the colours are beautiful, red, white and blue. The coffin was driven to our church. Then it was carried in by six soldiers from his regiment. The minister then said something like we brought nothing into the world and we take nothing out. I wanted to pray or something but I am so angry and I kept thinking but what about in between, my years with Tim? He's taking all of that out with him. Then we had hymns which is our kind of singing in church. And readings, poems, I liked those, I'll write them out for you some time. Then there was a tribute, like your praising but it is done by one person and we try to make it a bit personal, but not too personal because we can't offend anyone, so there was a lot about how brave he was and a hero and all that. I could have told a lot of stories about Tim and his old girlfriends and getting drunk together but there was his fiancée there. She's really down and upset but I can't get close to her. I don't remember much else, I was wearing one of my mum's black hats and it was falling over my eyes, we cover our heads at funerals, sort of the opposite to you.

They carried the coffin out to the graveyard and then I felt like you, I wanted to cling, hold it back from that horrible hole, but I just stood there, it was cold, maybe it was beginning to rain. Then there was one shot and the bugler played the music we call the last post. And that is the custom of our grief.

And then nothing.

TIME

ZARGHONA. Maybe only you understand, Emily but now I am angry with my brother. Isn't that terrible? He is martyr but I am angry.

EMILY. Yeah I'm angry. I think Tim was really stupid, all this business about being male and his mates, and living like a lion and even once he talked about defending our way of life. What way of life? Here it's everyone for themselves and bankers and bonuses. Please don't ask me what a bonus is.

ZARGHONA. Ajmal too talked about defending our way of life and I said our way of life is not good way of life, it is cruel and horrible to women, it is ignorant and full of hatred but Ajmal was angry with the Americans and the English too although he had loved English.

TIME

EMILY. Hey there. I want my brother back. I listen to music to get him back.

ZARGHONA. I would like to send you some Rabab.

EMILY. You might like Iron & Wine. It's just one guy who sings and plays the guitar. You should search him on YouTube.

TIME

ZARGHONA. Emily, we are so close and I only can talk to you but now I have to tell you. My brother wanted to defend Afghanistan from the English and Americans. Emily I have to tell you what I know. Your brother died by small fire at checkpoint in Helmand. My brother was also at that checkpoint that day.

EMILY. In a motorcycle accident?

ZARGHONA. A motorcycle accident is how we call it. Emily, the only way for my brother to defend Afghanistan was to join Taliban and he went to fight in Helmand. One of our brothers killed the other at that checkpoint, my dear friend Emily, we are also enemies.

EMILY. So this was some kind of trick, or spying or revenge or what? Do I care? In our country we call people like you bitches.

ZARGHONA. In our country we do have code of revenge and often the sister of martyr becomes martyr but that is not what I wanted. Is there code of revenge in your country?

EMILY. We let the Government do it for us, we are bombing you right now and I am not sure I mind.

TIME

ZARGHONA. Emily for days I have been trying to talk to you and I think you call it blocking, I am sending you new request. Please unblock.

Emily, I did not want code of revenge. We have a famous poem in my country by our seventeenth-century poet Rahman baba:

> 'Don't sow thorns; for they will prick your feet.
> We are all one body,
> Whoever tortures another, wounds himself.'

I could only talk to you and I hoped one day to visit your country and pay respect at your churchyard and if you come here you will be made welcome because we have code of hospitality.

I like to think our brothers in Paradise together playing Rabab and guitar, why is that not possible?

Emily, please respond. I want to tell you also because of the car they know my brother is Taliban and now we fear air raid or Pakistani police here and we have to move again. Please do not be silent with me any more. Got to Go

EMILY. Salaam

I've been told I can say this if I'm an old friend, I hope you don't think I'm being rude. I'm sorry I blocked you. There was so much stuff. But now I have no one to talk to. I miss you. I'm reading about Quetta and the birds. Tim loved watching birds. He would have been amazed by your eagles. Zarghona, please get in touch. Remember your dear friend Hi Emily, Zarghona please confirm this friendship request. Zarghona, where are you?

Sound of raid, last post, Rabat.

END